start living

The 6 week training
Extraordinary Instructions to Find Yourself

Manfred Winterheller

Translated from the German
by Nathan Ingvalson

Publisher Dr. Manfred Winterheller

© Copyright 2014, all contents, Publisher Dr. Manfred Winterheller, A-8010 Graz, Austria. All rights reserved.
This material including all of its contents is protected by copyright law. Any use outside of the limits of the copyright law without the publisher's consent is prohibited and punishable by law. This applies specifically to reproduction, translation, micro film productions, data storage and processing within electronic systems.
Publisher Dr. Manfred Winterheller
WINTERHELLER management GmbH
Rapoldgasse 22
A-8010 Graz, Austria www.start-living.com
2nd edition, 2014
ISBN 978-3902148186

to Uli

Table of Contents

Dedication 3

Acknowledgements 9

Preface.. 11

Prologue – The Aim of this Book... 13

1 Just do it – start living! 17

2 Changing Your Life is Changing Your Habits...................... 23

   2.1 Painful learning: stick with it until the bitter end 28

   2.2 Prudent learning: decide and enjoy.............................. 31

   2.3 More of the same: chocolate cake and fish soup............ 35

3 Why the Start Living! 6 Week Training?.............................. 47

4 First Dimension: The Goal 49

   4.1 Simply Do It 1: Find your goals.................................... 60

   4.2 Simply Do It 2: Concentrate on your goals, not on the path 63

   4.3 Simply Do It 3: Take your future seriously – where will you be 10 years from now?.. 70

   4.4 Simply Do It 4: Silence is golden – don't talk about it.... 72

   4.5 Summary 76

5 The Second Dimension: Trust and Confidence 77

   5.1 The royal path to freedom.. 84

   5.2 Simply Do It 5: Building confidence 91

   5.3 Simply Do It 6: Immerse yourself in your goals 99

   5.4 Simply Do It 7: Avoid energy vampires 101

   5.5 Simply Do It 8: Become a friend to your fellow man 111

   5.6 Simply Do It 9: Change the tone of your inner voice.... 114

   5.7 Simply Do It 10: Cut off the serpent's head................. 117

   5.8 In the meanwhile... 120

5.9 Summary 121

6 The Third Dimension: Persistence 123

    6.1 The difference between winners and losers 124

    6.2 Simply Do It 11: Decide upon something simple and follow through 130

    6.3 Simply To Do 12: The love letter project 136

    6.4 Summary 140

Acknowledgements

The totally new translation of this book into English provided me with an excellent opportunity to go through it again and to discuss many details. Now after finishing this process, I am both very grateful and pleased to say that I am still satisfied with the content. More than that, after many years of experience with the topics dealt with in this book with thousands of readers, many of whom have commented via email or personally when they attended one of my related classes at universities or in public events, I am more convinced than ever that the human mind is capable of performing real wonders. William James once stated that a man can change his life by changing his mind, and modern quantum physics has proven this to be fundamentally true. The impact of our thoughts on what we usually call reality is much stronger than what we believe.

At the very moment when we accept the wonderful truth that we are in charge of the happenings around us, we begin to recognize our real possibilities.

Furthermore, thoroughly rereading the book gave me the opportunity to think of the many friends who were facing some challenges during the time in which I originally wrote this book. It is wonderful to see that most of them chose very individual paths in their lives, making use of whatever they found reasonable from the time we spent together. By doing so, they followed exactly the guidelines found in this book. They designed their lives in a very personal way in order to enhance their learning and to experience more.

What remains unchanged is the meaning my family holds for me and my life. My wife and my four children support me in a way that gives more to me than I have until now been able to give to them. Usually we think that parents should teach their children, and this is indeed true when it comes to the basics of our social functioning, but when we leave this basic layer things tend to get turned upside down. The freshness of perception and the unconditional love I see in these five beings is something I deeply admire.

Together we struggle to find a way to live together as a group without limiting the individual. All of us have to find our own way, our very personal expression of the unlimited power that created us.

May the readers of all my books do the same. May the power be with them.

Love
Manfred Winterheller

Preface

Manfred Winterheller is the real thing. He says what he thinks and he does what he says, the doing here being the more important here. Thinking and talking alone lead to nothing. He has undergone many transformations. He received his doctorate in Business Management from the University of Graz, then went on to study medicine and took his oral exams. He spent years in academia working as an assistant professor. He is well versed in fiduciary and tax matters. As an independent corporate advisor and business manager of his own international software company, Manfred Winterheller has been intimately involved in everyday business life and leadership responsibilities for decades. He is also a family man. His wife and four children are at the center of his never ending growth and development. He invests his energies in the people closest to him, and receives the same in return.

Winterheller is endlessly setting new goals for himself. Whatever future vision he has in mind, he works to make it a reality. He sees himself running the Vienna marathon, and so finishes with a respectable time. He sees himself as a hip hop dancer, and he does just that during one of his software company events. He sees himself on stage playing rock music with his friends, and he makes it happen at the very same event.

He can draw from his rich personal and professional experience when working with people at his seminars who are seeking solutions for their problems. Winterheller has read a lot, he's heard a lot and he's seen a lot. He assimilates the impressions he's gathered and reassembles them into something entirely new.

I know many people who have abandoned their "habitual perspectives" after an intensive face to face encounter with Manfred Winterheller. Being crazy is not necessarily the same as being out of your mind. Being crazy can simply mean changing one's perspective. People who've worked with Winterheller have become physically, mentally and spiritually fit for life. They no longer pay homage to the demons of procrastination.

I also know many people who have not yet achieved their goals. It is for them that Manfred Winterheller has written this book.

Now is now. In 24 hours it will also be now, but a day will have passed... a day that is gone forever. In this way a lifetime can pass more quickly than a summer vacation. There are problems that are like a bungee cord – they are anchored in our past so we pull and pull until we reach the point at which we snap right back into our less than ideal starting position. Manfred Winterheller shows us how we can cut that bungee cord for good. We live in societies that provide us all with a precious gift: the freedom to choose our life's path.

by

Dr. Georg Reiser

Prologue – The Aim of this Book

It is the aim of this book to assist you in reaching your personal life goals; to reach a place in your life that makes you happy, allowing you to look back and be content with your experiences and what you've accomplished. This state is unique for each person. It fills you with the most profound sense of satisfaction, the feeling of having done well and being content with yourself. It accompanies feelings of comfort, peace and security.

Internally these states are similar in all people. From the outside the differences dominate. One person may be filled with the hope for adventure while another may hope for quiet and rejuvenation. People feel in harmony with life on a mountain or on the sea; they are happy when taking part in some physical activity or while making music. While some wish for professional success and extraordinary wealth, others strive for seclusion, circling the globe alone in small boats, or withdrawing from the world in the silence of a monastery for long periods of time.

Amazingly the mental mechanisms through which such goals are realized are always the same. Goals can be so very variable, nonetheless the fundamental patterns of thinking are similar; such thoughts are the indispensable prerequisites for reaching big goals.

For you personally, the specific goals you pursue are most important. In applying the techniques here, the exact aims are irrelevant. Whether you want to lower your golf handicap, increase your income or restore your good health, if you want to deepen your relationship with your partner or if you want to find someone special, the same three dimensions are always involved:

1. **Intention: You need a clear decision and inner commitment to a clear goal.**
2. **Confidence: You must trust in your ability to reach that goal and give yourself permission to do so.**
3. **Perseverance: You finally need persistence in consistently pursuing your goal and at the same time the strength and the courage to overcome any difficulties or obstacles.**

Your life is a movie in which you are simultaneously the director and the star of the film. A movie without the conscious creation of these three dimensions is boring and just fills time: it is a film without a clear plot and you are the main character who has yet to find a role. Through the conscious creation of these three dimensions you determine the continuing path of your life, regardless of whether you want to be a the best in the world at something or you want to free yourself from depression. As soon as you feel the desire to make a change in your life, to achieve some aim or free yourself from something, you have to activate these three dimensions in order to cause a new scene to show up in the movie that is your life. Then you've taken the biggest necessary steps in reaching a solution.

The Start Living! 6 week training allows you to realize these three dimensions, step by step:

1. Intention
2. Confidence
3. Perseverance

You'll be given clear tasks that you should accomplish in the six week timeframe. The tasks are referred to as "Simply Do It!"

This is a recipe that works with absolute certainty – simply "accept", or more accurately "act".

The training itself is easy to carry out. There are no secrets or mystical incantations – it simply involves "simply doing it". Nonetheless, it is not always so easy to do; only 5 or 10 percent of people actually work systematically on a successful life. You will be one of those 10% – but only if you recognize the avoidance tactics and the obstacles in reaching your life goals and defeat them. Recognize the danger – avoid the danger!

The first two chapters are dedicated to the avoidance traps in achieving your life goals.

The first chapter tackles the biggest killer of your life goals – waiting and indecision, feeling like a victim, and procrastination – the senseless hope that life will improve on its own. We make this killer of our life goals sound harmless when we use phrases like "I have to think about it". Thinking and not DOING! This keeps us stuck in place, allows us to stop moving and prevents us from making progress.

The Start Living! 6 week training can only be completed through action and not by thinking – this is crucial in your success in the training.

The second chapter describes the basic prerequisites which must be internalized: willingness to change, learning and taking responsibility for your life.

Then, with Chapter 3 we get to the point at which the training can begin.

1 Just do it – start living!

Start living today, RIGHT NOW! Stop waiting for some earth-shattering event that could change everything.

This nonsense has controlled your life for too long.

> *When I grow up...*
> *When I start school...*
> *When I finish school...*
> *When I have the right girl- or boyfriend...*
> *When I'm married...*
> *When I have a job...*
> *When I make some money...*
> *When I have children...*
> *When the children are out of the house...*
> *When I'm retired...*
> *When I'm dead...*
> *...and then it's all over.*

There is nothing in between, absolutely nothing. With all that waiting for some change that will be the start of everything, your time is slipping through your fingers. You probably have a tendency to analyze things, think things through thoroughly or – worse yet – you might discuss such things with people who have no more of a clue than you do when it comes to your plans. This is hardly ever the way to solutions, and on the contrary, only more problems, difficulties and dangers result. So, what do you do? You give up on your dreams and forget about them. You decide that they're "unrealistic", "childish" or "impractical". Once again you have buried a piece of yourself. This is a form of slow death that, bit by bit, will make you one of the living dead. When observed from the outside, you remain more or less a fairly well functioning part of your family, your company, your tennis club and all of the other obligations that you have to fulfill in your life. Inside you are empty and tired because everything that is fun is also dangerous, too expensive, only for other people. For you all that is left is responsibility and work. This is a bad situation!

Thankfully you can change that. NOW! If you say you don't have time right now, time enough to read a few more lines, that's up to you. When you are ready it will be NOW again. You will be a few days older, but nothing else will have changed. All of your problems will be waiting for you: patient, indifferent, constant. So the dumbest of all options is to procrastinate and to wait for each and every thing until it floats to you on the wings of a white dove.

The amazing message is this: You are ready and NOW is the time! Just do it!

> Within the next 10 minutes tell someone nearby something really nice. Thank the sales person at the bookstore for the good selection, the service or the atmosphere. Thank your partner for his or her

love, help and patience. If you are alone, call up a friend and thank him/her for something he/she did recently, for a kind word, a generous act, for his/her help. Call up your mother or father and express your gratitude for the millions of sacrifices that they made for you.

I know how difficult this exercise will be for you. Like most people, you are probably totally absorbed in yourself, in your concerns. You see no reason to thank anyone. You have the feeling that it's about time someone was nice to you. You have no practice in saying positive things for no reason at all. You have to have a reason, and today it can be hard to find such a reason. This is quite likely what's going through your mind. You think you should only be nice when you feel like it – only then are you being honest or "real".

Here you are mistaken. To be nice when life is good to you, when everything is perfect, when you feel good, that's no great accomplishment. Those are rare moments indeed when a frustrated fellow human being emerges from his cynicism, and for a brief moment he forgets all the wrong that life has done unto him. Such moments are as honest and as "real" as a dog's excitement when he's shown a piece of meat he'll soon get to eat. Now that's the truth!

The art of channelling one's life into a new direction, to being happy in a way most people cannot even imagine, lies in paying it forward, investing in yourself and just getting started. Earl Nightingale brought us these wonderful words of wisdom: In life most people live as though they were sitting in front of an empty wood stove and saying as soon as you warm me up I will give you some firewood, but as long as you stay cold, you're not getting any wood!!!

How much longer do you want to wait? Just do it! Throw some wood on the fire NOW. Start NOW with your new life.

> Repeat the first exercise within the next 24 hours. Find another person you can thank. You could thank a sales person who helped you out or a taxi driver who was kind and polite. You could thank the person working at a gas station who cleaned the windows of your car. This time don't just say thank you – give something more. Say something like "you really helped me" or "I am so pleased with the great job you did!"

Don't wait for some extraordinary, special treatment which seems worthy of special mention. Just keep in mind that you want to change your life, your own life, not the life of the person at the gas station. You are not to reward special treatment from others. Through this exercise, you and you alone start recognizing all that is so special or wonderful in your normal everyday life.

If ever you want to avoid doing an exercise, think of all the hope you have tied to reading this book. Think of the years you still have ahead of you. Think of all the experiences that you still want to have. Without a doubt you will live it ... if you keep at it. You might also experience it if you continue as before; but it will take you much longer. Every wasted day is a shame, so get going and just do these simple exercises. They take you out of your daily routine and the limiting thoughts that start with "Someday, when I...".

It is careless and unintelligent to simply believe what's written in a book, but it is also careless and unintelligent to not give things a try. Trying something does not mean believing something.

Testing is the only scientific path to knowledge. Only through results do we see whether a claim is true or not.

It is not enough to simply think about the results. ... *I can just imagine how this might work.* ... **The difference between thinking and doing is like the difference between night and day,** between rich and poor, healthy and sick, happy and unhappy.

Powerful thoughts cause action. Weak thoughts remain in your head and do not become reality. Powerful thoughts push outward and are realized, so when you carry out the exercises it means that you have had some powerful and intense thoughts. If you don't follow through with the exercises, it means that you have not allowed powerful thoughts. Powerful thoughts turn quickly into activities, events and things. Weak thoughts remain just thoughts for a long time and manifest very slowly, maybe even too slowly for the lifetimes we have available. Powerful thoughts can turn any situation around and achieve any desired result. The reasons for this will become clear to us later on – useful outcomes in your life only result from doing.

The Start Living! 6 week training works on the dimensions of intention, confidence and perseverance. You will see this again many times – intention, confidence, perseverance – dimension for you to build on and expand. This clearly means DOING, not just thinking. If you don't internalize this, you can put this book down and not give it another thought – thinking alone will not make this training happen.

Nothing comes cheaper than knowledge. Books cost very little. Scientists and highly educated people who have studied and learned (memorized) a great deal in their life often do not make more money than a skilled craftsman who left the education system at the age of 14. The crucial ingredient is doing. It is great to know a lot of things; it is even more wonderful to put them to use.

Take action! Take action now!

2 Changing Your Life is Changing Your Habits

In our Western culture we have a tendency to approach problems intellectually, and often enough that is well justified. Indeed, our highly developed intellect is an excellent source for finding solutions to many of our problems.

It doesn't matter if we need to solve a math problem or find a travel route for a trip, our knowledge and abilities, our memories of similar problems we have encountered or tips that we've read, the use of encyclopedias or the Internet can be of great help in taking care of a problem.

The situation is different when it comes to our most personal questions. Maybe it's a question of finding the ideal partner or the right job, or you want to stop smoking or lose weight – almost all of our highly personal problems cannot be helped using reference books or the Internet. It might be that there are no clear solutions, or if there are solutions we fail to implement them. You know what you would have to do, but for whatever reason you don't get it done.

Let's assume that we are more dependent on our habits than we would like to admit. Not smoking is a habit, just as is smoking. Once a non-smoker has passed a critical age where he or she is most at risk, it is nearly as difficult to start smoking as it is for a smoker to stop. Both are used to their behaviors and the related rituals. The comments made by non-smokers to smokers are just as stereotypical as the responses of smokers. Non-smokers overestimate the risks of smoking as compared to their own vices in the same way as smokers hope blindly that they will be fortunate and stay in good health. Both have a hard time changing their habits.

So if you really want to change your life for the better and be more successful, it will require changing one or more habits. This is more easily said than done. Psychotherapy tells us that people truly and lastingly change their basic behaviors, that is to say their habits, only under the most extraordinary conditions.

There is a good side to this: for one thing, habits simplify our life tremendously. Just like animals in the forest will use the same paths, a so-called game trail, we humans also tend to stick with behaviors that have proven to be successful. This allows us to not have to rethink or consider how we will get to the office, where our toothbrush is, how we should greet each other, etc. We conserve energy by sticking to proven successful strategies.

The other side of the coin is that we run into risks which are inextricably connected: just as the "game trail" makes it easier for predators to track their prey, our habits can bring about our downfall; they can keep us trapped in old life patterns. They can prevent our continued development. Such sticking to old, proven habits that we are attached to can go so far that change, or even the mere thought of change, can provoke a fear of change. This "power of the familiar" varies in intensity for each person, but is basically present in all of us and anchors our thoughts and actions.

This fear is countered by environmental pressure. We can see better possibilities than we can actually enjoy. We see the more beautiful, the better, the bigger. Television, radio, shop displays, catalogues, conversations with friends, nature – everything shows us the fantastic possibilities present in our world. In contrast, we suffer with certain things. Illness, loneliness, a lack of money, the wrong job, lack of understanding of our needs and desires in our immediate surrounding – the list of things which seem to hinder our growth seems to be endless. All of this works against our habit of leaving things as they are and urges us toward change.

We are caught between these two drives. On the one hand there is a habit which wants to keep hold of us. ... *Who knows what's next? It can't be that bad.* ... Old habits tell us about people who broke out of their familiar patterns and then something bad happened. ... *Be content with things as they are. It could be worse. Others are worse off and they don't complain.* ...

On the other hand we experience pressure toward change. It can't go on like this. ... *How many years* am I supposed to put up with this? I've had it! I've been sick of it for a long time. Enough! ...

Whenever you think about the pressing questions in your life you probably know this contradictory type of thinking: ... *I would like to change jobs, but I am afraid I won't find anything better. I am unhappy in my marriage but I don't know if I can risk a change. I would rather be self-employed, but what happens if I get sick sometime?* ...

In this place of indecision, most people stay fixed in place as if they're paralyzed. They do not realize that through this apparent not deciding they have made a decision: the decision to stick with the status quo and leaving things as they are now. Generally this is how our habits win out. ... *I hate my job, but I'm used to turning my personality off in the morning and back on again in the evening. I don't love my partner any more but we have some loans together so we better leave things as they are.* ...

It's strange. The staying power of our habits does not stem from the fact that our present circumstances are somehow beneficial. It is our inability to make a decision which actually stabilizes the status quo.

The chart below shows two opposing forces. One is the fear of change which is present in each one of us to a varying degree. It deepens our habits and prevents change. The other is the pressure imposed by current conditions that pushes us toward change and further growth.

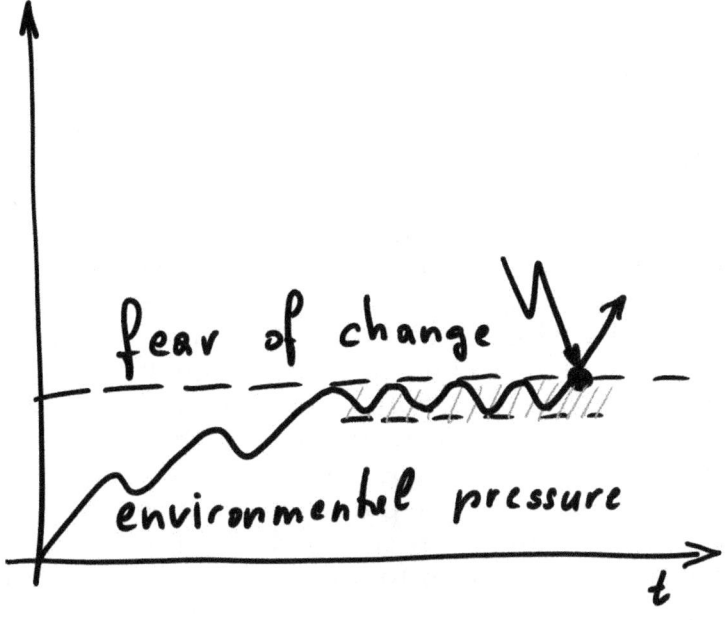

The diagram shows a clear point where the pressure becomes greater than the fear. At this point change becomes possible. From this there are two strategies which can be applied to the theme of change.

One can wait until the pain becomes strong enough, that is to say until the conditions become unbearable. This is the normal and most common method of dealing with difficulties: learning through pain.

One can reduce the fear of change and thus initiate change before things get any worse. This is the less common method: learning through prudence.

2.1 Painful learning: stick with it until the bitter end

Amazingly, we most often choose the path of learning through pain. We continue to put off change until the discomfort is no longer bearable; it is only then do we break a habit, like a butterfly breaking the confines of its cocoon. Sometimes butterflies/people wait for too long; they remain in their cocoon/habits for so long that they actually cease to exist. This might involve drugs, alcohol, smoking, being obese, being a workaholic or cheating on a partner. Many of us wait for that fateful day X when everything changes, for lightning to strike and to change everything. Good luck with that! The only thing that will come is greater pressure and with it a steady increase in discomfort. Every source of discomfort calls for a solution. If we put this off, the pain doesn't go away. We can try to get used to the discomfort, but sometime it comes to a point where we can no longer avoid it. It is then that we have to react. All those years of hoping and waiting were for nothing. Sooner or later there comes a drive to change.

Despite the gloomy prospects of this option, many people live in a state of significant unhappiness for years.

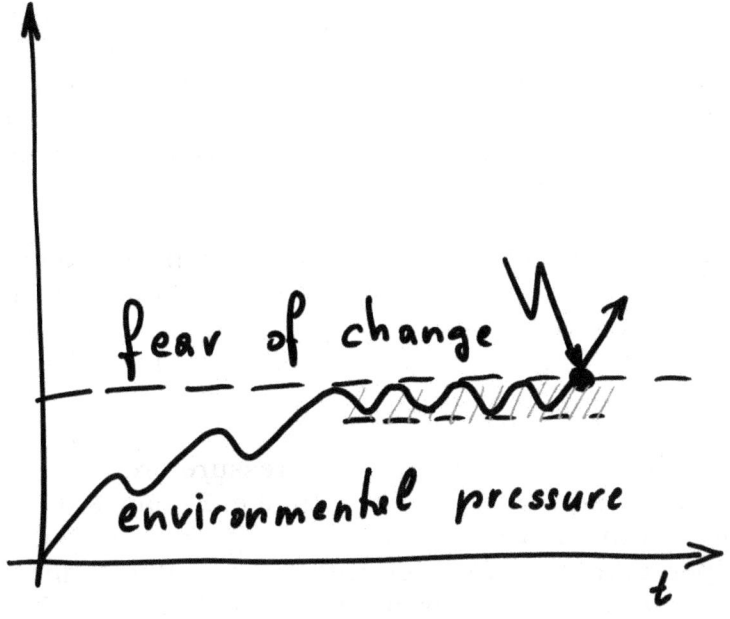

If the pressure increases until it reaches a threshold of change, this will first result in an intense anger and a strong desire to do everything differently together with the related proclamations. ... *It can't go on like this! I cannot take this for another hour. That's the end! I have watched this for long enough!* ...Unfortunately this will result in diminished energy, energy needed for change, and the internal pressure again drops. ... *I could do it anytime if I wanted to. One of these days I will do it – I'll change everything. Right now would be the wrong time. Maybe tomorrow will be better.* ...

This is how the distance to the threshold of change becomes larger again and change can again be put off. Why is this the zone of maximal suffering? If the pressure becomes even greater, enough that it simply cannot be ignored any longer, then the path to change would be clear and along with it the certainty of a better life would be in sight. If the pressure were any less, then by definition a more relaxed life would be quite possible. In this way, during times of uncertainty we swing back and forth between the knowledge that it cannot go on like this and the hope that a miracle will somehow happen for us.

If this is your technique then close this book. No one can help you at this point. Your reaction now is likely a call uttered by everyone who is unsatisfied and disappointed: ... *Why me? I don't deserve this. I try so hard.* ...

You will have to wait until the pressure grows, until you really and truly decide to make a change. Only when you have reached the point of such desperation, that any alternative is better than to continue on the present path, will you find a solution. Only then will it no longer be the way it was! Only then no one will be able to stop you from following your path to a better future.

2.2 Prudent learning: decide and enjoy

The second, and less common way is the path through prudence, the path that includes understanding of the senselessness of waiting. Sticking with the way things are, to what you're used to, is not a positive alternative for you. You know that the pressure will grow. You know that change is unavoidable. You know that change will be for the better if you are determined and follow your goals. This is how you will succeed in reducing your fear of change and taking the necessary steps at a point in time when the discomfort is still tolerable. You are not yet in a state of panic. You still have time to make decisions as to how your life should look from this point on. It doesn't matter whether this is a professional decision, a decision about your personal life or about you as a person. You have a lot more freedom and more available choices if you take action early on.

Learning through prudence is not an intellectual challenge. It does not require special cleverness. Surprisingly the most serious problems in life let us predict the ending without a need for any special kind of intelligence. A student who keeps putting off more challenging coursework, a businessman who constantly loses customers, a wife whose husband cheats on her again and again, an employee who is treated poorly in the workplace – all of them know what the end result will be.

The student knows that if he takes much longer to complete his degree, the other students in his program will be finished before he is; that in the end, if he wants to graduate, he will have to complete each and every one of the requirements. He knows that he makes it harder for himself and that the financial pressure on his parents will increase, and that questions from students he knows will become more and more embarrassing. If he closes his eyes to these facts it is not due to a lack of intelligence – it is because he shies away from the consequences of this knowledge. He has to be forceful and determined when taking a new path. It is not a question of intelligence, it is a question of power, the energy to make things happen.

The business person knows that his customers won't come back if he doesn't eliminate the reasons for their staying away. He knows that he cannot get a handle on this situation through cost control alone. He knows that sooner or later he will be standing there by himself in his store, because every employee will have quit as a result of all his cost-cutting. He knows that he has to take action. If he keeps putting it off, if he'd rather complain about bad times, blame his competitors, the political situation or the Internet, it's not due to a lack of intelligence; it is because he does not want to change. He feels tired. He thinks it is unfair that he has worked for years and now, just a few years before his retirement, nothing is working as it used to during successful times. He does not want to change anything. It scares him and makes him angry. He also needs strength and energy to take steps to make his life worth living again. Maybe he should close his business and use his experience elsewhere. Maybe he could change course – this is different in every individual case. However if he waits any longer it will surely be his downfall and he will not be choosing his next step, instead circumstances, the bank and his creditors will dictate what he does next.

The wife who has been cheated on knows that in the course of all her sorrow she will not become any more attractive, and that the situation with her husband will not change unless he falls ill, loses his job or has some other negative experience, when he needs readily available care or a shoulder to cry on, gathering sympathy for his undeserved fate. If her eyes are open, even a little, and she sees things as they are she knows that her husband will not change – not as long as he can count on her understanding. He sees himself as a victim of his drives, and in fact he would like to be different, without his wife he would be totally lost. All of that may even be true, and who would do his laundry or be there for him when he could not arrange a date with one of his girlfriends? Who else except for his wife would feed him the illusion of being a good father just for spending a few hours with his children on Christmas... until he had to return to his other "obligations"? Why on earth should he change? From his point of view he is in heaven. The only negative is the endless hurrying around, and the secrecy, but he'll just have to deal with it, his time well managed and always in sync thanks to his mobile devices. Yes, this is well known to every wife who accepted the first few affairs and all the related promises and oaths. She just does not want to take it seriously because that involves consequences. She would rather hope and not give up the illusion. She does not want to see the faces of her so-called friends who have to know by now and have to take care in how they word things. The problem is not a lack of intelligence, but a lack of strength and the energy to take action.

Then there's the employee who comes home every night feeling sick, who on Monday already can't wait until the next weekend; he can see where this life will lead in each of his older colleagues. Even when his resistance is tested at the counter, when everyone complains about the company and follows their own personal style of denial he can see that nothing will change. He can almost predict to the inch where he'll end up. He sees that his superiors, whose position he would like to inherit one day, also don't really have anything to say, that everyone has to seek permission for even the smallest decisions, that even higher up there is no praise, no appreciation, no common ground. Nevertheless, he hopes for the better – he only has to persevere. He believes that his coworkers would think better of him as a boss than of his current boss, if he could ever get to that point. This is not an intellectual problem. All the hundreds of thousands of people in middle management who sacrifice their lives to such senseless expectations are highly talented people who expertly solve difficult problems and are quite capable of making the connections. They do not want to accept it. That would mean they would have to make changes, give up some security, even though there is already certainty that they are wasting away as people. There is a lack of strength and energy to take decisive steps, to invest in one's own life.

2.3 More of the same: chocolate cake and fish soup

Behavioral scientist B. Skinner made the observation that pigeons, when given a reward, can learn a certain behavior very quickly and consistently. Kernels of food were thrown purely at random into the experimental cages, the so-called Skinner boxes which were named after him. When the pigeon inside the box observed the falling kernel, it began to believe that it had "magically" produced this kernel by way of its immediate behavior. Now, let's assume that the pigeon had just turned its head to the left when the kernel fell into the cage. From that moment on the pigeon turned left more frequently than before. This of course also increased the probability that it might be turning to the left precisely when the next kernel dropped (actually a complete coincidence). What was the pigeon's conclusion? It worked again! If we believe Skinner's theory, the pigeons then began to always turn to the left. It is fascinating to note that it is not even necessary that each turn be rewarded – on the contrary, it seems to be even more effective if not every attempt is rewarded.

This reminds us of human behavior. In the past we were successful with certain behaviors and now we can hardly leave them behind. Again and again we try to use the same methods. We have misplaced the keys. We look in the kitchen, on the shelf in the living room, in the black jacket from last night, in the blue pants we last wore and in the briefcase. Nothing, a lack of success. So again we look in the kitchen, on the shelf in the living room, in the black jacket from last night, in the blue pants and then in the briefcase. Nothing, no success. Now we are slowly becoming agitated. Where are the damn keys? Who has them? That's just typical – with this mess!

Where are the kids? Why can't I get help when I really need it?

We intensify our search and dig deeper – first in the kitchen, then on the shelf in the living room and so on until we get to the briefcase, where we find the notebook that we misplaced a long time ago, but no sign of the keys.

More of the same rarely produces different results. If you use a recipe to make a cupcake and mix all ingredients according to instructions, set the oven temperature correctly, pay attention to the baking time and spread on the icing, you will have created a cupcake. Maybe it's not a perfect cupcake, but nevertheless one could recognize your experimental cake. Never, and I repeat never, will you end up with fish soup if you make a cake. No matter how often you try, you will never succeed in ending up with fish soup. As a matter of fact you can expect that, sooner or later, you will be awarded for the ever increasing quality of your cupcake.

Well, why then would you try to change the results in this way when it comes to your job, or your personal life? Likewise here a specific input will lead to a specific and mostly consistent output.

Double the amount of input makes double the amount of the same output. The student noted above can double his intense avoidance of coursework, he can blame himself twice as much, he can double his hope for a miracle that he can avoid the upcoming coursework, but he will still be a lazy student. If the ingredients are not changed, the output – the results – will also not change.

Nevertheless, we can draw entirely different conclusions from our observations in life, and oftentimes we do so in mysterious ways. We believe that if we tackle the problem using the same recipe and the same ingredients, something entirely different will emerge. The employee does everything just as his predecessor did. He waits, he suffers, he hopes, he plans to do better. Despite this seemingly exact duplication of efforts he hopes for different and better results. He will be the ideal boss, relaxed, liked, highly paid. He believes he is the one who can create miracles. The same approach as that of his predecessor, long waiting, obedience, hard work, no time for his family, physical activity, friends. Everything is the same, but here is the difference: the magician speaks the magic words, and despite the fact that it's a recipe for delicious chocolate cake – fresh out of the oven comes a breaded veal and potato salad!

How can an adult who otherwise seems perfectly normal believe in such nonsense? How can the wife described above believe that she will create that one miracle with this unique therapy of simply waiting? She must believe that she is smarter, tougher and more persistent than everyone else. She has to believe that she will stay young forever, since she obviously does not calculate the years which are going to pass. She must believe that she will somehow win in the end, when her husband, if he has not exchanged her for someone new before then, will make up for everything when they're in their sixties. That's craziness!

Generations of young people have fallen victim to the fascination of such illusions. They are certain that they will do better than their parents on all fronts. Education, career, partners – nothing will be the same for them, no stone left unturned. So what do they do? They make absolutely no changes to their approach at the input end. To prove their independence from their parents they secretly smoke, ditch school, meet with friends – things that would be better that their parents don't know about. It is fascinating how every generation believes they alone have invented this resistance and that it is a clear sign of their being different.

Later on, when their own children come into the world, those early revolutionaries meet their children's struggle for independence with the same lack of understanding which they experienced themselves. Educational methods may have changed, but the basic convictions held by smart adults and dumb kids, refined by the process of socialization, have still remained the same. How will this go on? No change, forever the same. Same input – same output!

However there are always some who do break out of this compulsive cycle of repetition, who try out their own new way, something new. Usually these people are highly successful precisely because they decided to swim upstream. They made it, they chose their own path. Often, if they remain standing early on in their upward path, they are called "stubborn", or "headstrong". When the results begin to become apparent, public opinion begins to change as well. Luck and coincidence now enter into the picture. Connections are probably the real reason for their success.

Indeed, such people have mastered one skill better than the most other people: they have learned to learn. Not learning in the sense of memorization, but learning in the sense of a permanent, new definition of themselves as people and their own limits.

2.4 We need to learn only one thing: learning

Sometimes it appears as though we have to be stuck with our habits until there comes a point at which the discomfort is unbearable. We do not feel that we are capable of taking the required steps before then. All too often we keep things as they are. Blind and dumb, we hope for a miracle which can save us without any doing on our part.

The alternative to this is a changed approach to learning. That, of course, is more easily said than done, since our patterns of learning are habits which we developed during our time in school. We have to learn again how to learn.

What for? School is over and the career is moving along. You could argue that learning is naturally part of your job, or that you are one of the few people who buy more than just one book a year ... and you might even read it. You can easily remember how well you did in school; if it was good or excellent, then your ability to learn is proven, isn't it? If you did poorly in school, you will probably argue that in contrast to the students who put in a lot of effort, you did not invest much time in learning at all and you still came out looking good. The conclusion: your ability to learn is beyond doubt.

Let me rephrase this this in a slightly different way? Let me define the word learn from the previous sentence more precisely. It should read: your ability to "memorize facts and to recall them" is beyond doubt. You may have mastered this more or less thoroughly. Now add the ability to combine these facts and to think up something new.

You probably know that Vienna is the capital of Austria, or that the Caribbean has a number of islands and lies east of the American mainland. When your children ask you about this, you know that they have hurricanes there which destroy houses and can tear palm trees out of the ground, and that these hurricanes are given their own names every year, in alphabetical order. You also know that there are reefs there. Reefs? Aren't reefs those things in the ocean where colorful fish swim, Dad? Yes, exactly, that's where those colorful fish you have seen on television, green, blue, so colorful and so many kinds because of... Alright dad, how do you get there and when are we leaving?

Can you tell the difference between trivia and useful knowledge? A child hears something in geography class and wants to draw conclusions. That is an interesting place...that's where I want to go. You on the other hand, you know about it and that's enough. That's stuff we all spent time learning about in school. This thinking exists both in the way people are socialized and the way they're educated.

During my time teaching at a university, I repeatedly saw how students in a business simulation simply cut personnel costs without a trace of emotion in order to reach a desired result. I always pointed this out: my friends, those are people just like you and I. They live from the earnings of these jobs, and just like you, do not want to be unemployed. These are not simply some kind of expenses. They are just like you! For most students it seems unusual and confusing to hear this type of talk in an economics course and it makes many students feel confused. Many feel uneasy as now it is not so simple to implement such plans without giving this further thought. Nonetheless I don't really think my objections had much impact. Many think to themselves *"with this guy I have to be careful with the exam and give the right answer when the question about cost reduction comes up"*. They have probably tucked away my warning as just another piece of data to memorize, free from emotion and unchanged, just like they do with their other classes, i.e. personnel costs are almost always the first thing to be cut. So what? Memorize it and get it over with.

What good is it to relate to knowledge the way a computer does to a database, cold and emotionless, just like a teller at the bank counting the money? Wouldn't it be better if we didn't even know about temptations like the Caribbean?

Learning must have a completely different content. It has to touch our lives, each of our individual lives and those few years we have available. If, depending on generation and musical preference, you talk about Woodstock or Guns 'n Roses, or Mozart, you could probably talk about the topic for hours. Where is the passion you felt when you picked up an old guitar and played "I'm Going Home" from Woodstock or "Knocking on Heaven's Door", or you played the "Moonlight Sonata" on the piano like a possessed person? Why do you send your children to music lessons instead of going yourself now that you have the money to finally buy that saxophone you dreamed of all those years in your youth? Why are you waiting for retirement to travel the world? It's just like the thousands of crazy people who believe that they, barely making it past age sixty five, will still be youthful and beautiful, dynamic and creative. And all of that without any kind of exercise or healthy diet, of course. Do you really believe the promises of some miracle elixir made by advertisements where retirees hold hands and run through meadows full of flowers, or are driving convertibles along beaches? You have to be out of your mind.

I can already hear the arguments – you don't even have to say them out loud. ... *Oh no, I have to make money. I have to take care of my family. I can't just do my own thing. What will my parents and friends say?* ... Not to worry as we'll be addressing all of those arguments. We will look for solutions to these very real problems, solutions which can be executed and won't cause any harm, and will be so far from mainstream thinking that you – and this is a promise coming from experience with a countless number of people – you will be baffled by how you can find these solutions. For now let's stick with the topic of learning.

Learning begins when we realize that there is personal meaning. Whenever we learn something that we really don't care about, that does not affect us, we are just functioning at the level of a database. We are wasting our time, our lifetime. You're not working in human mode but in computer mode.

The two ways of learning:

1. **DB Mode (database mode):** fact oriented, defining, intellectualizing, thinking
2. **Human Mode:** result oriented, looking for meaning, acting pragmatically, doing

Useful learning, as opposed to the database mode, begins as soon as you ask yourself the most important questions:

... Why in the world did I spend so many years studying and learning if now I am only one of so

many, countless idiots who are insignificant little cogs in the machine? Why don't I control my own time? Why the hell do I have to ask if I can take my kids to the pool today? In school I had to ask if I could go to the bathroom – why hasn't that really changed? Why can't I make my children's dreams come true, dreams I understand so well myself. What am I waiting for? Santa Claus, the Easter bunny? ...

I can assure you, you can do more than you think. **You will fulfill the dreams of your children as well as your own dreams if that is what you really want.**

You bought this book because you want to change something, because you have this intense feeling that there must be more between kindergarten and the grave, more than what you have put up with for all these years, and which you can watch much like a long procession of boredom passing before your mind's eye. This feeling will not be disappointed.

With the help of this book you will learn how to learn. You will go diving in the Caribbean, and not just for a couple of weeks while on vacation. You will buy that golden saxophone and learn to play. You will cover Guns 'n Roses with your friends. You will be healthy and fit. You will shape up your relationship and whip your company into shape. You will find satisfaction for yourself and fulfill your loved ones' dreams and their heart's desires. And you won't leave this life until that happens.

Are you still there? Okay, it's best if we say it out loud: **"That's it, nothing can stop me now!"**

Stay tuned!

2.5 It's so simple?

It is not about being "so simple". We are not accustomed to conscious, useful learning in the human mode. It requires other ways of working. It is also more difficult and often more painful than database mode. Conversely, there are results which appear faster than you might expect and are better than you could ever imagine.

It's a good thing that it is so clear that every human being is capable of learning in the human mode. We are hard-wired for having these abilities. We actually apply this useful type of learning all the time, although we are unaware that it is happening. We constantly react to our environment. We only touch that hot stove top once. An emotional experience, pain, is so intense that we learn incredibly fast and what we learn stays with us. A single, small bit of information is enough and we understand.

I don't want that to happen ever again! Never, never, never again!

This feeling of "never again" is taken seriously. I never want to get burned again on a hot stove. It is just too painful. Indeed, we really will remember events like that all of our life, the effect of this "childish" oath is deeply impressed. Only in very rare exception cases will we get burned a second time in the same way.

The secret behind this is enormous pain. The pain leads to a totally clear decision.

I don't want that to happen ever again! Never, never, never again!

The difference between this and the intellectual observation that heat on skin can lead to a painful burn is more than clear.

Pain is an extremely intense sensation, the emotionally charged content is noticed quickly and the impression lasts. The decision is clear and it is final. No carefully worded formulation is needed. If it is easy enough I won't get burned again in the future. There is no I think..., I should..., If only I could. Those are all intellectual and thought based, rational and emotionless and we are not emotionally engaged. This does not lead to any results. The outcomes are just as weak as the decisions.

Many changes are based on a truly painful experience, an experience which has made it plain to see how urgently necessary the change has become. Never again!

It's great to know that waiting for pain is not our only choice. We can learn through prudence. However, such learning must be guided and accompanied by a clear and simple behavioral patterning which will require us to make small yet specific adaptations to our everyday life for a defined period of time so that we can truly stay on course.

2.6 Summary

Changing your life means changing habits. If we really want to change something in our lives, we must change specific habits. In order to change our habits and thus change ourselves and our lives, we have a very important thing to do: **learning again how to learn.** This means useful learning, and useful learning is results oriented! It is characterized by ACTION.

There are two ways to learn:

1. **Learning through pain.** This is the hard way – we do not make real changes until our problems, the damage and the resulting discomfort have grown so immense that we just cannot take it anymore.
2. **Learning through prudence.** This is the easy way. We can raise our level of awareness and realize what aspects of our lives are not the way we want them to be. We can gauge where certain things will lead and change course ahead of time – at a point in time where the discomfort is still bearable. This gives us the opportunity to think things over, to make a decision and to act. Our decisions will very likely turn out to be better than those we make under the pressure of great discomfort.

3 Why the Start Living! 6 Week Training?

To reach your goals, it is important to follow a few guidelines which will help you construct some new, successful habits. This involves a clearly defined period of time. For a short while you can follow some rules that are more strict because you know that it's only for a limited time.

It is much easier to hold on to good intentions and to reach certain goals over a measurable period of time than to change one's life forever right from the start. The need to make clear and lasting decisions is not made at the onset of the training, but it is a goal of the training.

In the course of your training you will activate untapped elements of your potential. Even mental giants such as Albert Einstein and Margaret Mead were of the opinion that they used less than 10% of their potential. Let's assume that our percentage is even lower than that. This means that we, in spite of doubling our abilities, are still way below the capabilities we have been endowed with by life.

Start living! is about the fact that we can overcome our limitations, limitations which, in fact, still sit within the comfort zone of our capabilities. The Start Living! 6 week training does not require any unimaginable revolutions, although the effects this training will have on your life will possibly be quite revolutionary. No personal sacrifices are required and the time period is manageable. What is important is persistence in carrying it out. In fact, even occasional forays into the world of the Start Living! training will produce results. But be aware that such results will lag far behind those which you can achieve with regular utilization.

The individual assignments, labelled "Simply Do It" in the training, are described in detail. You will receive clear explanations of their use and purpose. Some people do not need any reasons as they have the ability to follow instructions blindly for a while if they trust in the source of the instructions.

Most people from our culture seem to have an easier time if they can be involved in the process of critical and analytical thinking. They need to be able to understand how things work and the combined effects of the individual steps, not just on an emotional but also the intellectual level. To facilitate this, there is an explanation of what's behind each individual "Simply Do It".

4 First Dimension: The Goal

Where would you like to be ten years from now? What should your life be like? How much money would you like to make? How much time do you want to spend working? How should your personal life be arranged? Do you want to have a partner? Do you want children? What about your health? Do you want to live by the ocean, in the mountains, in the country, in the city? How do you want to spend your free time?

Have you ever addressed these questions, intensely and systematically, in order to bring clarity to what your personal goals in life are? Can you answer these questions clearly? Do you have an image in mind which you can call up as soon as someone brings up a time ten years from now?

Or has your life been such that you don't ask the question about goals in your life until there comes a time when you have to face disappointment? Was it sentimental and complaining, accompanied by the thought: What's it all for?

There is a high likelihood that up to now that is how you have handled things. People who really know what they want are quite rare indeed. Not more than 5 out of 100 people have a clear idea what they really want out of life. The remaining 95 only have totally unspecific ideas about their future: more money, more time off, less work, good health. Those are generally based on our common perceptions, noncommittal sentimentalities without any power. They do not activate real change. They do not motivate taking action. The energy of such common generalities will never ever be enough to really begin a new life.

You can easily test this out for yourself. If you ask the question again: how much more money, how much more free time, meaning when you take these sentimentalities seriously, then you will quickly see a retreat into the same kind of sentimental excuses: ... *it's not all that bad, one has to be content, others are much worse off, etc. ...*

Let's work from the assumption that you still don't know what you want. That's not bad. One of the essential observations of our mutual work here is the fact that it is not all that important where you are today. When tomorrow comes, what's happened today will be water under the bridge. What is important is the tendency of your life, the general direction. That is what determines where you will be in five or ten years from now. It would be bad if you just kept on muddling along that. It would be bad if you still had no clue where your life was going half a year from now. If you continued to wait for that sudden release, the bolt of lightning out of the blue and – miracle of miracles – sacks full of money emptied out before you, the man or the woman of your dreams appearing at your doorstep, getting rid of those extra pounds and finally a genie in a bottle who will grant you your every wish in the future.

Do you really believe in that stuff? No? Then why do you act like it? Why do you check off every day of your life simply in the blind hope that the following day will be better? Why are you so glad at the end of every day that "nothing" has happened? This kind of thinking can belong only to someone who assumes that only the worst can come from change, and therefore peers frightfully out of his or her armchair into the real world.

No, you must not be content with a life in which the best feeling is that of "nothing happening". From now on you should hate the days when nothing happens. Every single day for the rest of your life expect that something will happen, that things will shift for the better, that miracles do take place.

Remember your childhood, a time when every new day was a journey into a new adventure? Each day you helped good things to reign victorious. You were an American Indian or a super hero. You spent your days fighting evil, and beating the tar out of it every day. You were certain that without a doubt, one day you would be one of the best, the most beautiful or the richest people in the world, loved by your friends and by everyone. You were undoubtedly a prince or a princess, pampered by hosts of knights and servants. You lavished your friends with gifts and were feared by your enemies. What happened to that time? Where has your courage gone?

Please don't look at those images from your childhood with sadness. If ever there was a common characteristic found in all of the most successful people, it is this: they kept their childhood dreams alive. The content may have changed some, the princess became a successful woman, the knight may have turned into someone who today stands his ground. The confidence in the attainability of the highest goals unites world champions, leading managers, renowned scientists, the best doctors and successful entrepreneurs, with children. Where common people, those normal 95 percent, see only insurmountable difficulties, peak performers see exciting challenges which they will tackle with the same innocent abandon displayed by the children who claim victory over their imaginary adversaries.

It's easy to find out what kind of goals you have that meet these standards. Read the following questions quickly and without any type of deep analysis. Quickly give the answer arising from your innermost being, and while you are reading develop a sense of the two opposing types.

Joy-Rider	Normal
Do you have an idea what your life will look like in ten years from now?

Can you point out certain elements which you consider important?

Are you thinking of your income, your leisure time, your relationship, your health, your physical fitness and your relationships with coworkers, colleagues and superiors?

Will it be fascinating and clearly different from your life today?

Will you be richer, master your time, be happy with your partner with whom you've reached a good level of mutual understanding, be healthy and fit, be worthy of admiration and generous? | Do you think that it is better to wait and see what might happen?

Do you think that so much can happen in ten years and that it is impossible to plan as one might easily fail in reaching our great hopes and experience disappointments.

Do you know people who had this happen to them? People who boastfully wanted to reach new horizons and who are now broken?

Will you be content if you are more or less healthy ten years from now?

Will you be content if at least things are no worse than today? Do you think that life is not supposed to be fascinating? Should you be content and happy with that which you have been handed. |

Joy-Rider	Normal
Do you see any extraordinary highlights, things which define and distinguish you from the rest of humanity, things which you can be proud of?	Do you think the most likely high points of the next ten years of your life will be:
	Purchasing a new, economically priced television set
Is there a very specific mountain that you want to climb?	Buying a new living room set
Do you have an expedition in mind that you want to prepare for?	Taking a germ-free, all-inclusive trip
Would you work as an aid worker in a crisis zone?	If the opportunity should arise, a little affair on the side, but nothing serious – one doesn't really enjoy oneself without such diversions
Do you plan to spend time in a monastery to find yourself?	
Do you see that guitar in your imagination that you want to buy, or the piano, or the saxophone, Harley Davidson, or that red convertible?	
Are you secretly and intently thinking about a marathon you would like to participate in?	

Joy-Rider	Normal
Will you and your partner take a trip around the world, for a whole year, bringing home thousands of photos for that subsequent slide presentation which will take you all over Europe?

Do you look forward to now?

Do you yearn for novel experiences?

Can you hardly wait for your dreams to come true? Are you sure it will turn out this way?

Are there people with whom you can talk about your plans and who support your ideas, who encourage you and who are happy for you?

Are there people whom you cannot talk to about your plans, who would think you are nuts? | Could you do without those highlights if they were just to not happen?

Do you also have to be able to do without?

Do you never talk about your plans or talk about them only rarely because most likely it will just end up in a discussion about the possible and impossible risks posed by your plans? Do you think that it would generally end up in a discussion about all of the difficulties involved in living the world today?

On Mondays do you look forward to the coming weekend because then you get a brief break from your troubles?

On weekends, do you look forward to your vacation time because that's when you can finally get away from the daily grind? |

| Do you enjoy every day of your life?

Are you excited to get up in the morning, to see what new opportunities and experiences await you? | During your vacation do you find yourself looking forward to retirement because you will finally be able to start enjoying your plans? |

Do you see the difference? How does it feel, and what are your tendencies? If you are honest in your assessment, in what column do you feel more at home?

An enterprising way of living is marked by a feeling of enthusiasm, by the permanent search for meaning behind all everyday experiences. Life without change is scary to him. He needs the thrill, the adrenaline rush, the out of the ordinary. To the person with the normal perspective, this is childish and carefree, and maybe even irresponsible.

Normal people prefer an essential sense of security. Any departure from the modes of behavior and patterns of thinking he has developed during his educational years are frightening. He is most comfortable in a crowd of those who think just like him. To the Joy-Rider he seems inflexible, rigid, and above all he appears old, used up and dead before he's in the grave.

It is quite possible that you and your feelings can be found somewhere in between those two extremes. In many areas of your thinking and action you are adhering to your upbringing, or on the other side of the coin maybe you have been fighting this for years. In that regard, your behavior corresponds much to the one of a normal person.

On the other hand, maybe you have some hope for "something more", though not yet clearly defined, something better, something more beautiful. You can feel the triviality and the boredom of things that are forever the same. You sense that hidden deep within you lies another life waiting to be discovered, but due to a lack of support any such impulses keep getting hammered beneath the two main arguments of your life: How much would that cost? and What are people going to say?

Now is the time where neither obedience nor rebellion is a reasonable reaction. It does not matter whether you obey or rebel, as long as you just react as if you were still enslaved by the original influences. Now your goal must be to find your very own individual path which cannot be defined by agreement with nor by deviation from the public opinion; a path which does not require any justification except for the fact that it is your personal life, the fulfillment of your life's purpose.

You are unique, a select article of creation to add more of the joy of life and to contribute to ecstatic growth. This is not some mystical insight, instead it is a simple fact. The tiny oak seed develops into a huge oak tree, no matter how many other seeds may be scattered upon the ground. The offshoot of a rose will become a rose, no matter what other species it is grafted onto. Why do you copy your environment, your friends, or those idiotic "role models" presented on television?

From each crack in the concrete, from every crumbly piece of earth a flower will sprout, without care about its surroundings. Life presses on continually from each and every tiny crack that becomes available. Mother Nature is uninhibited realizing her building plans. She may adapt for the time being, only to work all the more intensively on her goals later on.

You will not fulfill your destiny if you develop as a copy of the world around you. You will miss your purpose in life if you attempt to be someone else, and you will miss your calling. Maybe you're not even copying anyone in particular. It is enough if you smother your inner voice, again and again, a voice which urges you to pay attention to your waking dreams, that voice which creates magic in your thoughts and ideas of a beautiful world, images in which you are loved, where the world is at your feet, where you are happy, grateful that you can exist in this wonderful world. There are images which let you sense what it means to be a child of an almighty and loving universe. If you listen to this inner voice it will become your internal compass, getting its orientation from powerful fields invisible to you that will lead you to your goals with unfailing certainty.

The first task of your Start Living! 6 week training is to listen to this voice, to give it an outlet. Just a small crack in the concrete of your thoughts is sufficient – it will awaken on its own.

4.1 Simply Do It 1: Find your goals

1. **Get yourself a notebook.**
2. **Every morning get up a half hour earlier and sit quietly in a place where you will not be disturbed during this time.**
3. **In this notebook describe yourself and also how you want to live in five to ten years from now.**
4. **Carry out this task every day for six weeks.**

Here are a few more additional instructions for this task; this will ensure your success:

1. **Find your goals, don't invent them.**
2. **Concentrate on your goals, not on the path that leads there.**
3. **Think long-term.**
4. **Do not talk with anyone about this process.**

These additional instructions will be discussed in more detail in the paragraphs below.

Your goals are an expression of your purpose.

Goals may be interpreted in different ways. It is possible to see them as arbitrary, as random decisions dictated by the trends and thinking of the times. Yes, indeed, it is possible that up until now you have only pursued those goals which have been dictated by others. He who has no goals of his own is condemned to taking on the goals of others, or serving the goals they have. A vast amount of mass consumption is based upon this aimless approach. If no individual internal measures for assessment are present, then we consider important that which others call important.

The right job or position, the right car, the right neighborhood to live in, the right outfit – these all become goals for which incredibly large sacrifices are made. Health, energy, enthusiasm, the joy of life, all these will take a back seat to keeping up with the Jones's and doing the right thing. Many people who have achieved things in this way have paid a very high price for it. They do not live the way they would actually like to live, instead they live the way as it is dictated by their circle of acquaintances. Spontaneously a similarly excessive counter movement has formed. Aimless living disguised as humility is preached as an alternative path. Deny your desires, think less of them. Be happy with what you have, even if it is far from what you long for.

Your goals should be more than just a superficial imitation. On the contrary, they should lead to your purpose, your place in life. Trust then that you do not have to create your goals in your thoughts. You must find your goals, not invent them. You may presume that your goals are like signs marking a path; they will lead you to your aptitudes and your tasks.

This is equally true for your material desires. It is a pathological paradox of our culture that the desire for material wealth is considered to be a moral aspiration which is not very highly regarded. It is not considered to be a special art to have many wants. Resignation however, is honored as being an extraordinary inner achievement. The Start Living! 6 week training does not follow this school of thought. If, after extensive work with your desires you arrive at specific decisions, if certain elements of your later life keep pressing to be in the foreground, this means that you have to fulfill a desire to do something in your lifetime. This realization of desires is your most personal task. It is not your job to ask yourself if the car, or the trip or the house of your dreams might be right for you, whether it might be morally justified or spiritual enough. Your task is to find your very own, inherent dreams and to consistently pursue them.

You are a tool in a much larger context, and your decision to make a purchase may trigger a process which you are yet unable to recognize. Maybe it is precisely your money which is needed to keep a business alive, providing the livelihood of a good number of people. Maybe your business partner desperately needs positive reassurance. Maybe he has doubts in his ability to maintain his family, maybe he's thinking about giving up. Of course this does not mean that you have to make a purchase for his sake. It just means that you do not know what role your desires will play in the course of the world's affairs. For this reason, if you come to know your desires within the framework of the Start Living! 6 week training, consider these desires to be messages from your subconscious, directional signs to your very own unique life path.

4.2 Simply Do It 2: Concentrate on your goals, not on the path

The goals you are seeking now together with the clarification of these goals you are working on are the contents of your future life. You are giving life clear messages about what kind of realization you are looking for. Don't ask yourself about the circumstances of this realization, the thousand little details which must come together in order to bring about the realization of your goals. The path, made up of the many individual actions which, all combined, will yield the goal. This path also includes the many difficulties that will have to be overcome. Remember that only when the goal has been clearly defined and charged with energy, when it remains permanently in your mind's eye, that is when the path becomes important.

Through the Start Living! 6 week training and by repeatedly pondering the question ... *Who do I want to be?* ..., you gain access to your purpose. Your goals and dreams are no accident; they are messages, information regarding the meaning and purpose of your existence. Did you know that you cannot intentionally force yourself to want something? Your desires come upon you, springing up from deep sources. You have not selected what you want. You can use it as learning material. You may peel away at it every morning, from your declared goals, from that which you have learned one is supposed to want. You will be amazed how this becomes more and more apparent to you. ... *I would like to make music with my friends.* ... At first you will be surprised. You must have other desires, a better paid job, a bigger car, an attractive and preferably young lover. ... *I would like to play my saxophone with my friends.* Oh no, that can't be. A saxophone, of all things. So expensive! Can't it be a flute, that would also be quieter. ... In a jazz club – in a smoky jazz club. ... Slowly you succumb to the feeling. It feels good to think about yourself in a jazz club with a saxophone in your hands. You can already hear one of your favorite songs and you can hear the audience applaud. Suddenly it is all crystal clear.

... I am going to play sax in a jazz club. ...

Suddenly you don't understand where this simple idea has been hiding all this time. You must do it! There is no doubt. And you suddenly also know: **Nothing is going to stop me!**

Maybe you also hear a completely different voice when you are writing. Maybe you catch yourself writing I would like to drive a red Ferrari. You cannot understand where this came from. ... *Idiotic. Useless. An unnecessary luxury. That's only for people who need such a thing. One reads about such needs. Not so long ago such an object of wonder was standing next to me at the intersection. That's it. Stop it! I can never afford that. No way. My friends would think I'd snapped. I would have to find a safe garage for it. I'm not parking it in the street next to my van. Damn, that's getting serious.* ... All of the sudden it really is serious.

... I'm going to buy myself a Ferrari. ...

It's as clear as day. It is inevitable. That's how it has to be. **Nothing is going to stop me!**

When you are lying there sick in bed, it might happen that one morning you write ... *I want to be totally healthy again.* ... Somehow this time it feels different than before. You have often complained –

yes, quite often in fact. Who likes being sick? Your visitors comforted you. Oh, it's not that bad. It will get better. But no one actually meant it. You didn't mean it either. Everyone thought – no, even worse – you thought ... *I'll just have to get used to it. ...* This time you write it without complaining, simply ... *I want to be totally healthy, completely, no ifs ands or buts about it.* ... Unfortunately the tests that came back were clear and the doctors have been straight with you. We'll do what we can, but there are cases where nothing can be done. Nevertheless, you realize that your desire cares little about the tests. ... *I want to be totally healthy again. I have a lot left to do.* ... Suddenly everything changes. You know. You're not hoping anymore. You know that you really and truly want to be healthy again. You are willing to do anything, make any effort, take on anything you have to take on. There is no going back.

... I am going to be totally healthy. ...

How could you forget? It's suddenly so simple. I am going to be totally healthy. **Nothing is going to stop me.**

Goals are an expression of your destiny. The ways to get there are only the means. The famous saying, "the path is the goal" does not actually go against this. In time you will learn to enjoy the journey to your goals. You will learn to appreciate it as the most precious aspect. But you will also understand that without a goal there is no path, only ways out. You will understand that an aimlessly lived life will only lead from one difficulty to the next. Every coast spans thousands of miles, yet there are only a few hundred yards of safe harbor in all of those miles. Without an aim no ship would ever find the harbor. Those who leave their ship to the wind and waves rather than to steering and direction cannot enjoy their journey for long; their thoughts tend to wander, seeking a direction to follow. But before "what" becomes totally clear, you already ask "how". ... *Who will pay for this? How will this ever work? Will my family let me do it? What will my partner say? How will my children react? How can I manage this with my job?* ... An endless litany of problems, big and small, seem to crop up and ruin every one of your ideas, no matter what those ideas may be.

Our reason can tell us that it is justified: what's the use of dealing with goals which, as it turns out later, are unattainable? So our rational conclusion is that every smallest notion stirring within us must be thoroughly examined for any possible points of resistance. This does sound efficient, and in some perverse way it is. The number of attractive goals drops down to about zero, everything would be difficult, expensive or dangerous. So everything remains the same, the habitual routes are taken and every risk is eliminated – except for the greatest risk of all: becoming petrified, losing sight of life itself, with our sights set only on difficulties in an almost addictive way. This will lead to the same fate that a tree suffers when it can no longer bend with the wind. That tree will be felled without feeling. It makes no difference to the wind; there is not a trace of aggression in its blowing. It is the tree which has become rigid rather than surrendering to the wind like the other trees, bending and quickly straightening itself again when it can.

Hence we must examine the opposite train of thought: what's the use of focusing on the path to a goal when I am not even sure if I really want it with all my heart? Isn't it just as logical to deal with the question of the intensity of our desire before we deal with the questions of implementation?

This will trigger an unexpected process. The more intensely we desire something, the smaller become the problems which stand in the way of its realization. Let's say that you have a very secret wish for a powerful motorcycle. As long as the desire is just a weak and rarely occurring dream, your head will start working on it every time: ... *You need a motorcycle license for that. That costs time and money. Riding a motorcycle is dangerous. You're too old for that. Don't be ridiculous.* ... Even completely trivial factors will come up: ... *Where will you park it? What if it breaks down?* ... The list goes on. It is a well-oiled machine working in your head. Mercilessly it beats down every one of your dreams – cruel, insensitive, uncaring.

The moment where everything changes is the moment you begin to recognize your wish or your goal, as being truly important. You change your attitude when a crazy idea, a pipe dream turns into a goal, a powerful image of your future life. Hoping and waiting does not make a future. This is powerless, without juice. The creation of your future must be a courageous and powerful process.

As soon as the idea of the motorcycle turns from a dream into a goal, a concrete intention, as soon as you begin to commit to this, that precisely this crazy idea is, in fact, something you yourself will turn into reality. As soon as you begin to smile at the thought what your neighbors will say, as soon as you begin to ask yourself which helmet you would prefer, if you want studs on your jacket or if that might be a little too much for your partner to handle. It's at that very moment that the problems melt away like snow in the warmth of the sun. Of course you have to get a license, but what's a few days or weeks training compared to the fun you will have going on vacation riding your bike? Of course all this costs money, the classes, the bike, the equipment – until you find out that the courses are much cheaper with a club membership. As chance will have it, you get a hot tip at the club office that someone has your dream motorcycle for sale, an orgy of steel and chrome, with exactly the picture on the tank cover that will drive people mad with envy. You solve the parking problem, and find a friend who, just like you, wants to spend the summer in Italy. And that's only the beginning. As soon as you have caught on and see how this works, the mechanics of your life so to speak, you will realize one dream after another – you'll see. It always works in the same way. Listen to your inner voice. Let it speak. Don't swallow every idea that comes up. Produce a powerful inner image, and experience how one thing leads to another.

Right from the start, simply accept the idea that you carry amazing and crazy goals within you. They don't all have to be realized. Just let yourself be carried along. Take notice of all of your crazy ideas, everything you have suppressed for decades, just allow them during that half hour in the morning. Some goals will not survive this six week period. They are not important enough; they might resurface later on, or maybe never again. However, some of your goals – actually more than you think right now – will gain momentum. They will grow into amazingly realistic intentions that create energy and press for actualization.

You will begin to recognize that you carry more enthusiasm within you than you ever thought possible. You are younger than you think. You have all kinds of strength and energy. Where the heck has all this been for all these years? Where have these impulses been hiding? How have you been able to stand the daily grind for so long? No perspective and no hope except for looking forward to a somewhat bearable television program? You'll realize that you only survived this lifeless existence because you did not know what you were missing – the pain would have been unbearable otherwise. You'll also see how empty your life has been without this energy, how unloving you have been, how little you actually contributed to creating a better life, a better world for the many people who had no idea what is possible and what they are meant to be. You'll understand Freddie Mercury and Queen: **We are princes of the universe, born to be kings!**

4.3 Simply Do It 3: Take your future seriously – where will you be 10 years from now?

We live in a thought tradition which puts the status quo before the future. We are used to first asking ourselves ... *Where am I now?* ... Only then do we ask ourselves ... *Where do I want to be?* ...

And with this question "where do I want to be?" we tend to prefer a short-term perspective. This makes us skeptical about our goals. In a short period of time, we no longer trust ourselves with real changes. We almost tend to necessarily take steps that are too small, which we logically justify with the need for interim goals, the need to remain realistic, etc.

Let's put a stop to that! Anything that is realistic is trivial, ordinary and boring. Anything that is realistic is already prepackaged, sterile and wrapped in foil or available in the form of colorful catalogues for mass marketing, chewed over a hundred times over and predigested by the real pioneers who were doing things at a time when the notion still seemed unrealistic. Realism is the worst type of fiction there is. Realistic is always that which already exists. Realistic is the ordinary, the daily grind. Regardless of how terrible something might be, how stupid, trivial, uncaring or inhumane – if it exists, it is realistic. Almost anything we consider to be obvious today, what we take for granted was totally unrealistic just a few years ago and people considered it crazy. Today, organ transplants are an everyday occurrence, a reality for anyone. A few years ago the first transplant surgeons were laughed at because of their ideas. If the doctors in the past always stuck to what is realistic, our toothaches today would still be treated with a wooden block and a hammer. It was always the unrealistic that expanded our understanding of reality. It is always the pioneers of the mind who dare to think up things which seemed impossible to the normal mind. They define what is realistic. We, the skeptical, watch their initial difficulties with a grim sense of satisfaction. They seem crazy to us, stubborn and unteachable as they stick to their absurd ideas, and justifiably so. The farther these pioneers' success in learning does reach, the more their ideas seem to be feasible, the more they become known to everyone. Just a few years later, the masses then demand their share of what has now become commonplace.

If you give your goals a bit more time, if you think in time segments of five to ten years, you will also be more courageous. It's clear that over a longer period of time, more changes as well as greater and more revolutionary transformations are possible in your life than those that can happen in the next six months.

4.4 Simply Do It 4: Silence is golden – don't talk about it

When a thought gains energy it develops a tendency to manifest. It pushes for implementation and seeks realization. This natural movement of a growing, strengthening thought is perceived by most people as an unfamiliar pressure. Talking seems to be a way to alleviate this pressure.

Lessening pressure can lead to a weakening of the power of a thought. Talking prevents a sufficient amount of energy from gathering, energy that in turn can result in a true breakthrough. Only silence about the process can lead to excellent results, even if there is only a small amount of initial energy. A weak thought, like a small creek, will at first give no clue as to the powerful energy which it can have once it is dammed up. Also, in a small creek, the amount of water that is available is normally small. Well-behaved, the creek stays within the confines of the riverbed that has been established over many years. Once an obstacle hinders its flow, if tree trunks or branches begin to dam up the potential power of its water, the tremendous energy grows. If the pressure of these forces is relieved soon enough by removing the obstacles from the creek, it will swell temporarily but will remain in its bed. A few minutes later everything is the way it was before. Only if an obstacle is present long enough, if a truly significant volume of water begins to collect and forces its way out of the old creek bed to eventually sweep the obstacle along, only then does it become clear what enormous force can be developed even by a small creek.

The development of the power of our thoughts works exactly like that. Normally they trickle in uninterrupted sequence through to our conscious awareness. None of them remain with us for long enough to grow and develop. Moreover, we likely repeat negative thoughts. Insults or fears resurface repeatedly in our thoughts until they ultimately have garnered true power and they gradually begin to manifest more and more clearly in the form of illness, depression, hate, rage, etc. We don't usually cultivate constructive thoughts to this extent.

The Start Living! 6 week training is a true exception here. It focuses our thoughts slowly but surely on our desires, that which moves us innermost and propels us toward growth, health, partnership and wealth. In this way you stick to constructive thinking much longer than you would ordinarily within our normal rhythm of thinking. If we keep interrupting the process of developing power by prematurely talking about our goals, always dispersing some of this yet insufficient amount of energy, we will not be able to powerfully break through our usual patterns of living. There will again and again be some positive tendencies, but they will not lead to truly important changes in the end.

Getting stuck in the process is very painful. It feels like something is tugging at your life. Repeatedly, there is pressure to reach for something new, to make some tangible positive change in your life, but again and again the old forces win out, pulling you back into the possibly hated but nonetheless familiar track. There is a rise and fall, an ever alternating sense of hope and the recognition of many possibilities, followed by a regular experience of disappointment when nothing comes of the promising initial progress.

That's why there is a simple and highly effective commandment: Silence is golden.

Talking about the process and its effects has yet another serious disadvantage. Most of the people you talk to will pounce upon your enthusiasm like vultures. They will use this little bit of energy they have at their disposal just to destroy your slowly developing ideas and your still fragile plans. It is easier to destroy a house than to build a new one. It is easier to smear over a picture than to paint a new one. The destruction of entire forests can take place in a matter of hours, but rebuilding such a place will take hundreds of years. That is why people with weak energy prefer destruction. ... *That will never work. How did you come up with that stupid idea? Do you really believe that nonsense? Why should you succeed? Do you have any idea what this will cost? What will your family/your company/your boss say about that? Many have tried such a thing before and failed. Don't be ridiculous!* ...

Such remarks have an especially profound effect when they come from friends, people to whom we have close emotional ties. Such cutting remarks will affect you deeply. This is precisely where you find the biggest danger to your efforts. Of course you don't talk about your goals with people you don't get along with. Just the opposite. You talk almost exclusively with people who think well of you, who want the best for you, people who you love and who love you. These people don't want to cause you any harm. Nonetheless they do just that with thoughtless criticism. It doesn't matter whether a vase is intentionally or accidentally knocked off a table. Whether your goals have been trampled intentionally or unintentionally really makes no difference at all. There are people who need just that kind of response for a challenge, who will use the opposition of others as a means to "show them", to straighten up and draw energy from this. That said, the majority of those doing this exercise will do well to avoid this kind of run in. Give your goals time to develop. If you have built up the mental energy, if your goals appear clearly before you, then there will be the time for conversation. Then you will be able to smile at your voluntary advisory. You will no longer argue unless you need help or support. The unsuccessful theoretical discussions about what works and what doesn't are no longer your concern. Dogs bark and the caravan moves on, that's your attitude. You will pay the next round for your friends who know it all, and you will leave the place amidst a thankful round of applause.

4.5 Summary

Simply Do It 1: Find your goals. What do you want to achieve in your life? What would be the MOST fun? It is not even important here where you are today. What matters is the direction you begin to move in from now on! For the next 6 weeks, take a half hour every day and write down your goals. Describe yourself, how you see yourself in 5 to 10 years from now. Describe how you want to feel, what you want to be doing – professionally, personally, with your body and creatively. Describe how you want to live, what qualities your relationships should have, etc.

Simply Do It 2: Concentrate on your goals, not on the path. Write down something every day that's like "a letter to Santa Claus". Think only of that which you WANT and your goals. ANYTHING is possible. All thoughts dealing with how to get there are not allowed! This technique will enable you to FIND your real goals, the ones present within you, rather than just finding some kind of goals.

Simply Do It 3: Take your future seriously. Where will you be 10 years from now? 10 years is a long time in which endless things are possible. This will allow you to be more courageous, and you won't think right away about what's "realistic". Realistic goals are boring, and are given up on automatically anyway. Instead think about your real desires – things that make you deeply excited.

Simply Do It 4: Silence is golden. Talk with NO ONE about this process, especially not about your goals. The probability of losing this newly built up energy through talking and/or from the comments made by the people you talk with is very high.

5 The Second Dimension: Trust and Confidence

Among people's more fixed convictions is the idea that reaching a goal depends on a number of different preconditions: relationships, rich parents, luck, education. The most varied things are made use of in order to shirk the responsibility for one's own results in life.

According to the viewpoint of the mass mind, which is the sum total of the beliefs of a culture, an individual's fate is not in the hands of that individual. Many people feel that they are at the mercy of life and that they are completely helpless in the face of life's ups and downs.

It stands to reason that under such conditions, our own goals will likewise be seen as being very difficult to reach. There are too many unknowns that can topple our plans. We really can never be sure if some event might prevent our success.

In order to support working on our goals it is therefore important to change these basic convictions. Life must be lived as moldable. Again, this is why the Start Living! 6 week training includes some very concrete tools, referred to as "Simply Do It", which will get your mind ready, step by step, for the infinite opportunities present in your life.

It is important that we trust in life. Without trust we will be paralyzed before every single step. Not to trust makes us cautious. Before we can make any decision we have to peek around a thousand corners as without trust we can never be sure that there isn't danger nearby. Without trust we do not dare to look forward, to get excited, because we fear that life will play tricks on us and will vengefully take it all away again at the peak moment of our joy. Without trust we do not dare to love for fear of the pain of loss. Because of this we approach every relationship with caution and hesitate at the smallest risk. Even in situations where no risk is perceived we fear there might be one, well hidden or camouflaged. How can a joy for living develop in that way? How are we to taste the richness of life if we are expecting pitfalls everywhere?

We must trust in life. Only when we trust in life do we feel trustworthy ourselves. Only when we trust in life can we recognize, accept and enjoy its numerous gifts.

The art of building trust in life is thus an indispensable prerequisite for a happy life.

The much quoted remedy of positive thinking is simply not enough if you want to make truly fundamental changes in your life. The prayer wheel type repetitions of positive affirmations seeps into your thought processes so slowly that you may never really reap their benefits.

It's better to start at a deeper and more fundamental level. Albert Einstein is credited with the observation that the most important question in every person is this: does life love me? Resist giving a quick answer. This is not a matter of rational evaluation, but the deeply rooted picture from your childhood and youth which later almost confirms itself and removes everything that doesn't fit, and therefore seldom changes.

It's about the deeply rooted feeling about whether you were brought into this life and delivered into a wonderful paradise or into some type of hell which has to be suffered through. Pay attention to how you immediately react to this question. If you had been asked this question just now with a microphone and camera pointed in your direction, how would you answer?

Could it be that you are looking for the middle path, that you find arguments for both sides, for the paradise version as well as for the hellish version, and would you therefore claim to be undecided? Could it be that you say we all create our own worlds? Everyone makes their own luck. Everyone lives in their own self-made heaven or in a self-made hell? That would mean that you're mostly going along with the current trend in thinking. There are no absolute truths. Much of the Start Living! 6 week training touches on precisely these principles. It's in your hands. You can steer every situation in another direction. No matter what the situation is, you are the master of your fate. All of this is right and it's been proven millions of times. Nevertheless, this is not an answer to the initial question: **Am I loved** by life? The question still stands if we realize that we can influence our destiny. Only when you have made clear and definite decisions will you be able to see a clear and definite course for your life.

It is not a matter of theory, or general connections. Our intellect would prefer for us to remain noncommittal and undecided. But running away from the answer will not get you anywhere.

What course is likely for your life if you are so undecided about the most important question of your life?

This is a solid fact: the answer to the crucial question "Am I loved by life?" will determine the course of your life. There is a solid connection between your attitude toward this question and that which you will face in your life. This connection is so clear that you can get your own inner answer from your life itself.

If your life takes on a very unsettled course, if moments of success are always followed by moments of deep desperation, if you continually have the feeling that you are on the edge of a breakthrough, that you've almost made it but then it fails to happen, then you haven't made up your mind about your answer. It is a rough mixture of the feeling that you are loved and the fear you feel in the face of life. You are under the impression that you have to earn this love. If you try hard enough everything will go well. Nonetheless you know from your childhood that is it very difficult to ever try hard enough. You are always making some kind of mistake. Something always goes wrong. You cannot manage to break out of this cocoon. The atmosphere is scarcely okay, and some misfortune turns up and it starts all over again. Most likely the key to your understanding of creation is the word "volatile". There are actually connections between your actions and the consequences which result from them, but they are not really reliable. There is always the uncertainty that even the best of your intentions won't be recognized and also not rewarded. Life always has the random power to present you with big problems. If you don't overcome those problems, and almost more importantly if you are not grateful for them, then life will punish you again. You experience life as a constant test, a suspended sentence, and you can never be sure if you will be able to ascend to greater heights. This is equally valid for your professional life as it is for your personal happiness. There seems to be nothing that lasts. There are always unforeseen events. On the one hand, they are well-deserved consequences of your lack of skill so far, and on the other hand a chance to finally prove that you deserve success and to live with peace and contentment.

It is understandable that this unending threat, the perpetual insecurity about what can still happen today, will not allow you to experience any true inner peace. Every ring of the telephone can mean new difficulties. Every letter can be a catastrophe, in the worst case it could be a notice that you've been fired from your job. Do you know the feeling you get when you receive a letter from the government? The feeling that immediately comes up: what did I do wrong, and the relief when it turns out to be only some harmless official notice. If there is a policeman at the side of the road, all approaching vehicles start to slow down, even those which were not driving over the speed limit. Lasting fear is our constant companion.

Are you loved by life, you personally? As long as you cannot answer yes to this question without reservation, you will never be truly happy. Our whole life long, from the days of our earliest childhood, we long for someone to love us unconditionally, to always forgive us, again and again, no matter how often we err.

We are looking for friends who understand us, for partners who will stick with us through thick and thin. When you were a child you always wanted to be held, protected and loved. To be loved when one does everything right – where is the art in that? To be loved when one has done everything wrong, to be loved when one is full of self-reproach, to be loved when one wishes for nothing more than to take back all of the mistakes, that truly is love.

This feeling, though widely praised by the whole world, is largely unknown. How many times does "I love you" really mean "I need you"? Test yourself sometime as honestly as possible. If your partner wanted to leave you, would you be able to help him or her to create a new life? Simply because you wish that he or she should have a good life, you want him or her to be happy, without reservations, without accusations, without expecting gratitude in return? Few of us are capable of this. Most likely we would shower her or him with complaints, let them know how ungrateful his or her behavior was towards you, how much you sacrificed for them, how often have you denied yourself for the sake of the relationship. ... *Is this the thanks I get? Do I deserve that? This is how I'm rewarded. If only I had known?* ... The list goes on. Not a trace of love is visible in this. It is only my needs, my claims, my demands. Even our seemingly unselfish actions often spring from the hidden motive of seeking to secure either the gratitude of that lucky one or establishing ourselves as almost saints.

As we don't really know what unselfish devotion is, we tend to go on the assumption that life is either indifferent, or in the worst case life has some negative motivation. If we are good, then life will treat us well. If we make mistakes we will be punished. Somehow we sense that this is not such a good deal, but we accept it as a given. That's just how it is. We live in a cruel world that can strike fateful blows any time. Nothing is certain, our bodies are threatened by illness, our incomes may disappear into nothingness at the whim of the boss. It is through innumerable coincidences that we are healthy when we get out of a car or an airplane in the evening. Even under the best of circumstances we are threatened by the decline of old age. Decrepitude and the need for long-term care are apparently the unavoidable outcome of our advancing years. All that does not sound like paradise.

Can you see the connection with your inner perception of yourself? If you do not feel loved by life unconditionally, your inner perception will take on the title "not worthy of unconditional love". This leads to a whole series of consequences. You will again and again attract events that confirm this "not worthy of love" scenario. To compensate for this you start activities to prove the opposite, activities that aim to show that you are "worthy of love". Due to the overwhelming effect of your self-perception, the failure of this filtered image has been preprogrammed, causing the original program to be upheld, and it even becomes reinforced. The only way out of this endlessly self-perpetuating vicious cycle seems to be that we become hardened, we give up, so we don't have to bear the constant disappointment.

5.1 The royal path to freedom

The real and lasting path to freedom is the decision for one simple thought: I am loved by life. I am loved in a lasting and consistent way which surpasses any amount of love we humans could ever muster up. Life forgives everything, over and again. We cannot even really imagine that. We are so deeply caught up in the notion of guilt and atonement. We have deeply internalized beliefs like an eye for an eye, a tooth for a tooth. We have been told that our every thought and action has consequences, and since many of our thoughts and actions are less than loving, we subconsciously expect the inevitably resulting punishment.

I am loved by life means that I can trust in life. Moreover, I can trust in life blindly. It doesn't matter how difficult my situation may appear at this moment. If I am loved by life then it will free me from every difficulty as soon as I let go of the problem. If I am loved by life, it will grant me the fulfillment of my wishes. Life supports me in this way, and life shares in my happiness.

I am loved by life means life knows no guilt. We might err a thousand times over, we might falter ten thousand times, yet life will see past this completely. It is not capable of punishment. It is not even capable of forgiveness. Forgiveness requires awareness of something that has to be forgiven. Life does not take notice of our missteps. It sees only us, its creation, and is proud of this creation in whose hands it has given incomparable power.

If you imagine parents who love their children unconditionally, who are always and without hesitation on their children's side, then you may get a small sense, a tiny notion, of how much you are loved by life.

> Next time you have a premonition of some impending doom, decide to have this attitude – just as a test. Ask yourself: if I were my own only child to whom I am deeply attached, and if I had the power to determine the outcome of this event, for what would I decide? Now take the very best decision you can think of, the most wonderful results which seem thinkable to you, and rest assured: precisely that and likely something endlessly better is what life wants for you. Life is so much more generous than we will ever be, so much so that we cannot even imagine its gifts. Life gives and gives and gives. If you internally ask yourself the question why have I felt so little of this up to now, you will recognize that you haven't yet accepted this. You were afraid and had a bad conscience. You did not dare to ask, out of pure fear of being rejected. You thought that it would be better to ask for nothing, to hope little and above all, not to attract attention. This alone was the reason for your path so far. Now, let's put an end to this. Do the test!

If you are ill and are afraid what the tomorrow's findings might be, do the test as described. What would you wish for if the door opened and the greatest capacity for healing in the world was standing in front of you and asked you what you would like most. Would you have the courage to say ... *I want to be healthy again, completely healthy. I wish that nothing would remain of this illness, nothing at all. I want to be able to completely forget about my illness. I want to erase it. It should never have been. I want to walk again, run, jump, sing, dance, love, laugh again, just like you. ...*

Do you have the courage? This one step, you recognizing deep down inside you how much you want to be healthy again, is the determining factor on your path. Not the way it has been up to now, when you were willing to take all the problems upon yourself with a sense of guilt, bent beneath your burden. Of course you wanted to be healthy, even before today, but, was that really a powerful decision you made? A decision as it is suggested here, a clear, unequivocal demand, backed by the certainty that you will, in fact, receive what you wish for?

Would you beg your father or your mother ... *Oh please, stay with me. Don't leave me alone in my misery? ...*

No, if you could be sure that you would be helped, you would shout: ... *How wonderful, that you are finally here!* ... Without question you would go pack your suitcase. Not for one second would you doubt that your misfortune is finally over. Precisely this type of certainty is what you will bring to life now – just as a test.

If you have financial troubles, decide for the same process. What is your deepest wish? Would you wish that this horror were over? Would you like to wake up from this horrible nightmare? Could it be that you would love to be free from financial troubles, want to have enough money put away so that you could finally rest peacefully again?

Do you have the courage to say ... *I really want to be successful at last. I know that I am entitled to more than I have enjoyed until now. I want to feel good again. I want nobody to have a lack of money. I want that things go well for everyone. ...*

For financial concerns, this last part of your request is especially important. If it is about good health, it is quite obvious that health is not a limited commodity; theoretically all people could be healthy at the same time. If a person is healthy, this does not mean someone else has to be ill. We've learned something else when it comes to money: wealth seems to be a limited commodity. If someone becomes rich, it's as if someone else has to become poor. As long as you believe in such nonsense you will never be able to be rich. This is because if life had invented this cruel nonsense it could not love us. What father, what mother would intentionally prepare too little food for their children and then watch them fight over it? As long as you have such perverse ideas in your head, you will be unhappy. Being rich requires the courage to put an end to this type of thinking. Just observe nature in its incredible richness and splendor, how much abundance there is displayed, day in and day out. Billions of blossoms appear every spring, and billions of fruits grow from these blossoms. When it rains, it rains in great abundance. Generosity is the measure of life. Diversity commands all that we see. Only our human greed creates bottlenecks and artificial limitations. As soon as you decide – just as a test – that limitations are no longer acceptable, not for you and not for anyone else, your life will take a turn as you never thought possible. If there is enough, then why hoard? If there truly is enough for everyone, why take something away from someone else?

Observe even your subtlest thoughts. As soon as you create limitations, as soon as you think that some people actually don't deserve something, and rightfully so, because they do not work enough, are too lazy or whatever the reason, as soon as you permit your ego to get in the way, you begin to create limitations. Generosity is the best and most effective form of self-interest because it is based upon the feeling that we are loved by life. As long as you feel you have to watch out for what's yours, you have not understood why the birds in the sky don't plant and don't harvest, and yet they thrive.

If you are alone and if you sometimes have the feeling that you will never find a partner who is compatible with you, do this test. What would you wish for if you could know with absolute certainty that your wish would be filled? Do you have the courage to demand the ideal partner, the man or the woman of your dreams? Here, too, lies an important trap. If you would like a specific person, then it is possible that you have excessively restricted the outcome. That particular person may well have other goals which do not necessarily have to be in harmony with yours. There is a clear and distinctive difference between goals as they relate to other people as opposed to goals which are related to things. Generally speaking, it is a good idea to attach "or something better" to the end of your goals. This is particularly appropriate for people who follow their own individual goals based upon their own awareness. It is possible, however, that you might end up forcing your goals upon another person so you cannot be sure that you will actually attain your own goals if they involve togetherness, closeness, a sense of security, mutual support, etc.

If you believe that you absolutely have to have a certain person, you are expressing in this need that there is only this one person for you. Hence you succumb to narrowness in thinking. You see life's opportunities as being limited, especially if this person is already otherwise engaged, if he or she has already decided to be with someone else, then this narrowness in thinking can hinder the fulfillment of your dreams. Only if you wish for every person to have the partner of their dreams will you find yours. Don't ask why so many other people have happy relationships, people who to you don't seem to be very loving or nice. Every person has different challenges. Your challenge might appear in the area of loving relationships and so it is in this area that you will have to make a special effort in order to realize the love of your life. If you had several children and you had to decide which ones should be happy and which ones should not, wouldn't you give the same amount of happiness to all of them? If you love your children would it be conceivable that you would exclude some of them? If you now make this test and decide to see life as being more loving than any one person could ever be, is it still conceivable that you are destined to be alone, unhappy and lonely? No, of course not!

Now do you see the connection to the first fundamental element of finding your goals? In the morning you define your goals within the framework of your assignment of finding your goals and the feelings connected to them, and with the second element of building your confidence you fortify your conviction, that you, in fact, are entitled to these goals and feelings.

It should be becoming clear that it is worth deciding to correct your inner self-image. Such a correction promises results which will make your wildest dreams come true. A positive self-image draws positive events with the same kind of strength and power as we know is the case with a negative self-image. Wealth, health, partnership, happiness, security, anything you want to wish for will simply flow into your life as easily as it did before in a negative way. Especially if you think your situation is too desperate to make a change, or impossible to induce a radical and total reversal of the situation, you can now look to your future and be at peace. If you were powerful enough to attract problems into your life, you are without a doubt also powerful enough to get rid of those problems. There is no doubt about it.

5.2 Simply Do It 5: Building confidence

1. **Get rid of your television set.**
2. **Do not read the newspaper.**
3. **Stick with this assignment for the next six weeks.**

There are some additional instructions for this assignment to ensure that you are successful.

1. **Use the time gained to have conversations with the people you love. Be actively involved in your family life.**
2. **Use the remaining time to read magazines or books that deal with subjects involving your personal goals.**

Actually, it shouldn't even be necessary to discuss this any further. The alternatives are obvious. You have more time for your partner, more time for your children, more time for your friends, more time to yourself and for your goals. Nevertheless, you will possibly find it difficult to accept these two restrictions even for the brief period of time that the training requires.

Let's be clear: this is not about a general change in lifestyle. It is not about the overall banishment of the television set from your living room, or the suggestion that you no longer busy yourself with the news. It is about a brief period of catching your breath. You need time for the Start Living! 6 week training to reorient yourself.

Togetherness instead of television.

As mentioned above, this is not about the television set per se. It is simply about the brief period of time of the training. More would be hard to ask for. Your television set most likely has the best spot in your living room. Like a shrine it has been set up directly across from the couch, so that its present devotees can adore it without difficulty. If you were to give up your television set it would leave a terrible void. You would sit there with your family or your friends, staring at a gaping emptiness. Everyone would be grief stricken by this enormous loss. You would really miss it. You wouldn't even know how your friends on all the TV series are doing. The discussions in the office about yesterday's program would have to take place without you. You would have to stand there blushing next to the coffee and pastries – you don't have a television set. You might even be avoided for being a weirdo and labeled an outsider. Your children would be mocked and made fun of in school. You would have to respond to the rumors that you could not afford a television set!

No, no, no. This training is supposed to help you, not burden you with additional problems. For just a brief 6 week period you are to talk to your partner again, listen to your children again and chat with your friends. You are going to find out, most likely to your great surprise, that the teenagers who sometimes sit on the couch next to you are your children. It is incredible how time flies. You turn on the television while your kids are still small, then a series has barely been shown for the third time around and the kids are grown up. You could experience similar surprises where your partner is concerned. Yes, he or she is still there. Whether he or she still knows who you are, who can say for sure?

Your conversations have probably been mostly about organizational things for many years now, about the evening meal (... *Don't wait for me – it will be late.* ...), about the need to buy a new washing machine or a new car (... *Again?* ...) or about incompetent politicians and football coaches (... *They don't have a clue, but no one asked me.* ...). You will look around where you live and you will discover astonishing things. Much has changed since you have taken your inner leave of absence. You will find that there are families in real life, too, and not only on television. They also have some real concerns, but if someone says something there is no round of laughter in the background. This all may seem sort of strange at first, but keep in mind that it's only for a short time.

When was the last time you listened to your partner? What moves her or him? Do they still love you? What kinds of feelings do you have? Certainly, people get used to each other and it is normal that over time this sense of closeness falls by the wayside. But is there something left? Once upon a time – it sounds like the beginning of a fairytale – when you absolutely adored this person you longed for every call, for every small sign of affection. You were jealous of anyone else's look. You even – God that was so long ago – wrote letters which were full of all kinds of promises and vows. Were you stupid then, or are you just stupid now?

> **Sometime** today give your partner a gift. Right now. Stop reading. Reading doesn't change anything. Just do it! You don't know of anything he or she might need? You are wrong – he or she needs you! You're not in a relationship? You are wrong – you have a great number of friends. You have been sitting around feeling sorry for yourself for too long. Call someone now and say I'm coming over. Buy a book, some music or flowers – rush to the nearest supermarket and buy some wine and cheese, olives, or cake and coffee and then go see

your friends. You cannot possibly get away right now? Send an email, a telegram, order flowers, call or send a fax.

You see no reason for gift giving? That's not even necessary. You don't need a reason. It isn't about rewarding someone. You should be simply nice so that you will become happy again. This is how you start. It is not even necessary that the lucky object of your attention is going to be happy, grateful, or will learn something from it. **This is about your life,** your one and only life. You are sending an impulse. You don't do it to be praised. To be honest that would be a poor reason. You are changing the course of your life. Now, for a brief amount of time you decided to change from being a passive bystander and a couch potato to being someone who acts. The others are probably still sitting on their couch in front of the TV and are happy that way. You might be one of them again soon enough. But first you'll want to know if out there – in the real wilderness – if there is life without television.

It might take some time to reorient yourself at home. The kids, just like you, are no longer used to family members talking to each other. For a long time communication was limited to only some brief remarks. ... *When will you be home? Where are you going? Did you do your homework? Why do you need so much money again? Why are you so late? Clean up your room! Put on some decent clothes! Look at you! What will the neighbors say?* ... It is possible that your children have passed up the deeper meaning of these remarks. It is also possible that your kids simply think of you as old, tired, used-up, clueless and disinterested. Maybe your kids cannot stand to hear the constant lament "I am doing this for you" any longer. It is possible that your kids have tried to get through to you, to talk to you about their problems, about their disappointment with their first big love, difficulties in school or many of their incredibly important experiences which will never happen again after those first seventeen years.

You were not there. Physically you were there, in fact even more of you than before in terms of weight. In your thoughts you were very far away. At some point you crawled off into the land of worry. Barely through the door and you switched on the television to tune out. You were not even aware of the evil double meaning of this tuning out. At home you shut (yourself) down and were not even present for years. If someone had a problem you would have to switch yourself back on, you would – in your own words ... *never have any peace and quiet at home. ...*

How much easier has it been dealing with those stupid, artificial problems of your friends on television, or getting upset when you listened to the news? Unnoticed by your otherwise perfectly functioning reason, you are duped into such things. You started to swing between two extremes. Plane crashes, trains derailing, rapists, women abandoning their newborn babies, floods, avalanches, erupting volcanoes, wars, accidents, killings and assaults. On the other side are the television images of the wealthy and stylish, palm-lined beaches and dream cruises. Vacations, vacations, vacations, money, champagne, affairs, intrigue, drama, sex without worries, Porsche, Ferrari, Jaguar, yachts, traveling the world and the games of millionaires.

Both are equally unrealistic, focusing on excerpts of the world and ignoring the other ninety-nine percent of what happens. If news reports were to give us a realistic view of the things that are going on, if anyone would be interested, then news programs would have to report on the wonders of the world for more than twenty-three hours a day, telling us about the millions of airplane passengers who get on and off airplanes unharmed every day, and even more train passengers who safely travel to work and back, men and women who work hard for their families, and about parents who make every sacrifice in caring for their children. The daily miracles in nature, the cherry blossoms, birds circling above forests, crocuses in spring, that is real life. In 24 hours of programming, only the last ten minutes before midnight would be needed for catastrophes.

It is understandable that the media mostly DOES NOT report on real life. If people were actually interested in real life, they would only have to go out of their front doors. For this reason, the media has to focus on the exceptional; that is why exceptional events will continue to make their way onto the news – the more perverse and inhuman, the better.

In the mean time if you look clearly at your surroundings, you will first look at it through the learned filter of the media. If one day your children want green hair, you will automatically remember everything you have ever heard in the media about "those" children. You will not immediately realize that you have been told only about the exceptions. There may be countless young people with unusual hair colors who never find their way onto television programs, simply because they are normal, nice young people. Who thinks of such subtle nuances when agitated. This is how trouble starts.

Your children may be under the impression that you are not even aware of them. He or she has no interest in us. Your children would like to talk to you, tell you things and ask your opinion. Children and young adults appreciate the opinion of experienced advisors, but only if that person takes genuine interest in them and doesn't just rattle off their prepackaged monologue. Young people can't talk to most adults, and if you yourself have ever truly entered the incredibly fantastic world of your children, you will understand that. ... *If only I had the same opportunities. I had to work really hard. I never cheated in school. We never ditched school. We were happy and grateful. No alcohol, no kissing in the hallway, no being late. ...*

Like a wind-up toy, you endlessly repeat the same lies. The only good thing is that they are not true. I do hope that you occasionally cheated, and I'm sure that you ditched school sometimes, faked an upset stomach, and put away your first beer before your fourteenth birthday – contrary to all of your "I'm such a good person" claims. About those kisses in the hall – do you really think you will earn applause for presenting yourself as the biggest bore in the world? Do you think that someone will admire you for the fact that you were too much of a coward to get close to those girls you liked so much, or for not even making an attempt? Are you really that old and out of it that you don't understand how much prouder your children would be of you if you finally told them how you tried to steal cherries and then had to spend half the night up in the tree because the farmer's dog was in the yard? Can't you see that your advice is urgently needed when it comes to that first heartache, or that your help is needed for a math assignment that has been put off too long and is now hanging over your kid's head like the sword of Damocles?

Listen to your children today. It is easier than you might think. Just close your mouth. Incidentally this is almost as if you were watching television or reading the paper. If you can't stand it anymore, if you think you have to say something, keep your mouth shut. All you have to say is "okay", "really?" and "that's interesting". If you think you need to give advice: keep your mouth closed. If you think it will kill you: just keep your mouth shut. At the end you say: "Thanks, it was nice to have this talk with you".

And if you find after some time that your children start bringing their friends home rather than going somewhere else, and when, for the first time without being asked, your children say that they are glad to have a mother or father like you because the other parents don't understand their children so well, then sneak off into your bedroom, fall on your bed and cry a little. It hasn't been easy to come this far, but you have at least kept the vow from your childhood: you did a better job than the generation before you. You are a friend to your children. Few parents can come close to that.

Give yourself a chance, just for six weeks. Give yourself six short weeks to become young again.

5.3 Simply Do It 6: Immerse yourself in your goals

This assignment serves to increase your level of trust. Get to know the wonderful aspects of life. You will learn that there is a real world here which offers us fantastic opportunities. To do this you will concentrate on the world around you, on the people nearby. Not everything will fill you with joy. You will discover some things you wished you had been able to prevent earlier on. But at the same time you will be amazed at your personal impact, the unique effect you bring to your personal environment. There actually are some areas in which you are irreplaceable.

From this foundation you can now work on your goals. Instead of reports of catastrophes which deliver the negative and distorted, and sometimes even an extremely warped image of the world, you will follow the many opportunities which are available to you to reach your goals. The most important places to do this are book stores and magazine departments. You will see that all the knowledge of our human world will be at your fingertips, and practically for free.

Invest yourself consciously in magazines and books that have to do with your goals. If in the morning, while writing in your journal, you ponder the thought of riding your motorcycle through the Sahara, you should begin by getting a travel guide and then go on to motorcycle magazines – anything that seems to you to fit somehow together with this dream. If you want to catch the fish of a lifetime, then read all about fishing. From salmon in Alaska to big game fishing in the open sea.

If you are a business person or you are dreaming of a career in management, read the memoirs of famous managers. You will learn that all of these extraordinary personalities had to make it through some very tough times. To your amazement you will read that the typical winner is primarily defined by his ability to deal with disappointments and defeat. The same is true for the best athletes in the world. Many of them had a truly bad start, seemed completely unfit for the athletic discipline in which they later became world champions or Olympic medalists. You will find that many coaches think that particularly talented people often have to face greater difficulties than the average beginner in achieving their extraordinary performances. This is because the average person has to work harder right from the start, and moreover must face disappointments and discouragement more often early on. Talented people may achieve huge success very quickly and then topple over at the first big problem due to feelings of self-doubt as they experience a temporary lack of success in a particularly strong way. They suffer to such a degree that it can prevent them from finding the connection again. This is how a temporary lack of success turns into permanent failure.

The stories of successful people will give you great courage. You will learn to recognize the greatest common fallacy: the belief that success is a gift, a talent, which some receive and others do not. You will begin to recognize that success equals hard work – hard work not only in the sense of training or long work hours, but more in terms of overcoming difficulties.

5.4 Simply Do It 7: Avoid energy vampires

This assignment is for increasing your trust and is likely the hardest task of the entire process. It relates partly to you personally and partly to the people who surround you. It must be carried out decisively but also with care.

This assignment is intended to be carried out only during the training period. However, it will hone your understanding of the mental components of your life and may thus clearly affect the organizational aspects of your future life.

1. **Make a list of the people with whom you have regular contact.**
2. **Differentiate between friends and vampires; mark each name with either an "F" for friend, or "V" for vampire.**
3. **Avoid the vampires and use the time for your friends.**
4. **Don't forget your own name on the list. There is no one you spend more time with, or deal with more intensely. Behind your own name mark a "V".**

Of friends and energy vampires

The difference between a friend and a vampire is not a matter of good or bad. It isn't about people you love or who love you, or those to whom none of this applies. It is not a matter of difference between people who want to harm you or help you. None of the traditional categories apply here, and therefore it is important that these groupings are well understood.

Vampires are people who, for the most part unintentionally, rob you of your energy and enthusiasm. The full name for this species is energy vampire (vampirus energeticus). They are people who have some type of criticism for every one of your ideas. This is not because they have focused on the problem intensely and have recognized various risks, but because primarily they can only see problems and difficulties.

You go out in the evening with some people you know. Everyone is joking and chatting until, with perfect regularity, somebody begins to complain about something. It might not even be something which concerns the person directly. It might be something he read in the newspaper, saw on television or heard on a radio report. He begins his rant on the subject and is immediately joined by some others, and then either an argument erupts or, which is more frequently the case, he contributes something negative to the conversation. After a short while the whole group is caught up with a topic that begins to escalate. It progresses from political issues, on which the participants of this conversation are of course much better informed than the stupid and corrupt politicians, on to business, the chaotic traffic, exorbitant taxes, and eventually the ozone layer. Everyone has something to contribute which fits with the general mood and which is something like this: nothing is working, everything is getting worse, you cannot trust anyone, everything is too expensive. It's a shame, but unfortunately one can't do anything about it.

Are you familiar with such evenings where you get home and you are dead tired? You are completely exhausted and probably think it´s the late night and the drinks you had.

That's not the case. Just compare this state of exhaustion with an evening after a hike in the mountains or after a long run or a day trip on your bicycle. You are physically also very tired, possibly even quite exhausted, but you feel happy inside. You have had a truly intense experience, have pushed yourself to the limits, but you have gained strength. You have seen what you are capable of. You sit down with your friends after it´s all over and you experience the day once more. You remind each other of special moments and you feel that you have had a full day.

The exhaustion you feel after that first described evening out is internal. You are burned out. You are demotivated and feel incapacitated. Maybe someone even made the mistake of bringing up an idea that was fascinating for him. The whole group then came down on him and his nonsense. ... That will never work. That's expensive. Much too dangerous. Nonsense. ...

Most likely everyone there knows someone who has tried the same thing, or something roughly similar, and experienced disaster. Nobody knows exactly why, but it definitely went wrong. Maybe others have read about someone who tried something really different, and it also went badly. The stories outdo each other in their general descriptions of failed projects. Only one person never gets a word in, the initiator, the person who brought up the idea in the first place! He is pretty shocked as he first thought that his suggestion was actually a good idea. He wanted to discuss it with his friends, get a little support, and maybe polish some of the rough edges. Of course every project involves risks, and it would be good to recognize these risks early on, but that the whole idea is crazy is news to him.

Energy vampires live off the energy of others. Like everyone else they need ideas, initiatives, and enthusiasm, but they do not develop these ideas themselves – they prefer to steal them. They suck the enthusiasm out of the people they talk to. They only see difficulties. They are masters of destroying energy and are proud of their gift of quick understanding. With lightning speed they recognize how to kill an idea: ... Have you thought of this? You have to do something else first. It will never work that way. I have thought about that too, but I considered it a little more thoroughly than you. ... Their killer arguments are endless. They are no good at reasoning and it is not their role to encourage something, to support, or to improve. They embody the verbal derailment of a spirit exclusively aimed at destruction, because that is when they can experience themselves as being important.

Just like Count Dracula rises from his tomb at night, lusting after fresh victims, an energy vampire thirsts for your lifeblood. He needs this energy to survive, although he is not aware of it. He has made destruction a life principle. He is proud of it, because he sees his criticism as a contribution to the discussion. No one is quicker when it comes to dissecting ideas with razor-sharp reasoning, analyzing weak spots and eviscerating them with pleasure, like a fresh kill on a hunt. The energy vampire will only deal with failed projects. He wishes good luck to successful projects, as in his opinion they will need it. In his world, failure is eternal and success is only a temporary event for naive idiots. If you bring up successful people, he will point out that you cannot see behind the surface: even those people have their weaknesses somewhere. With a knowing glance the vampire sees into the future, and what does he see? Ruin, failed hopes, defeat, illness and death. When the sun is shining brightly he will remind us, like the seers of old, that rain will surely follow. If the sun still shines tomorrow, he will make his prognosis with only greater assurance. Then, with the first drops falling in the weeks to come, he will be satisfied. He knew it all along.

This description might lead to the erroneous belief that vampires are easy to recognize and that they are bad people who don't wish any good upon others. This kind does exist: cynical, know-it-all, grumpy and frustrated. There are also others who appear to be the opposite. There are people who really wish you well and who want the best for you. They want to protect you. They wish you all the fun you can have, they just want to prevent something bad from happening. They look for weakness in your ideas and do so out of love and caring.

If one day you were not completely healthy because you hurt yourself playing soccer with your friends, these people will come to see you and cry at your sick bed: ... Wom, how could this happen? You look terrible. Are you okay? Well, that's what happens when we get older. It will surely get better. ...

Actually, you felt pretty good and wanted to use this time in bed to recover and get back on your feet soon. But now you start to worry. ... *I look bad? Am I getting old? What does that mean "it will get better"? Is this injury really that bad?* ...

You did not think for a second that this injury could have something to do with your age. Actually, you were quite proud of your competitive spirit and your commitment. But now you are beginning to wonder. ... *Is it possible that I might not have injured myself doing the same thing a few years ago? Wouldn't it be safer to play chess?* ...

Maybe you can think of some other occasions when you felt weaker than you did a few years ago. ... *When I run up the stairs I get out of breath quite quickly. If I eat too much, I get heartburn. I never used to have that.* ...

Do you see the effect of the vampire? Where has your courage gone? Where are such idiotic thoughts coming from? Watch the vampires – they recover during these moments. As you (the sufferer) get weaker, the color usually rushes into the pale faces of the vampires. Suddenly they have the strength to comfort you: ... *Don't take it so seriously. That's how it goes. It'll be okay. I'm here for you.* ...

Try a test next time. As soon as you see a vampire gathering energy as described above, you recover too. Say something optimistic, get your energy back. Say, yes thank you, I am sure it will be okay. I am so glad that I have you, and next week I want to play on the same field and shoot more goals than ever. Now watch how the vampire becomes very attentive. He fears the loss of easy prey and is afraid that you might want to get your energy back. So he will begin to suck again. ... Well, it won't happen that fast. If it's not better, you're still recovering. A relapse is worse than the illness itself. What if it turns out worse next time? ... He will only be happy when you are down on the ground again, when you look to the future with pessimism, and when you have let go of all your hope.

These "loving" vampires are more dangerous than their cynical counterparts. They are harder to unmask. They are also harder to fight. While you might be able to tell an ordinary vampire occasionally what you think of him or her, you feel helpless against those "caring" vampires. They make sacrifices for you. They are worried about you. They mean well for you and only want the best. Whenever someone brings up the argument that he wants only your best, look out! **You don't want to give away your best,** you want to enjoy it yourself. Anyone who wants your best wants to steal from you.

Even caring vampires are vampires. The effect is the same: loss of energy, falling enthusiasm, initially only for the projects discussed, or rather destroyed, and later a general loss of motivation.

Over the period of your Start Living! 6 week training you should avoid any contact with energy vampires. Avoid meeting. Say you are too busy, tired or you're going on a business trip. In this vampire-free time, or at a time with fewer vampires, you can then recover.

It is possible that some of them will threaten to withdraw their love. ... If you don't have time for us we won't call you anymore! ... Thank your stars that it is so easy to get rid of the energy vampires. As soon as you are no longer willing to provide your regular blood/energy donation, those vampires will look for a new victim.

And you, in celebration of the event, can hang a wreath of garlic in your hallway. Yeah, that's that!

And what are you yourself, friend or vampire?

The question is answered quickly. You yourself are the worst vampire in your life; additionally, you cannot hide from yourself. There is no excuse so you can get away from yourself. This energy vampire, you yourself, is almost invincible. Almost!

It might be helpful to first check if the basic term actually applies here. Let's take a simple example. You are standing on the tennis court during an important game which will determine your acceptance onto the club team. How are you handling yourself? Are you paying attention to yourself, do you have calm and positive courage? ... *You are doing great. Sure, you'll make it. If you don't, it's no big deal. Your chances are good. You made a couple of mistakes, but you are getting better all the time. You're getting more into the game, next come the points!* ...

Or do you analyze yourself and your preparations with the scrutiny of a vampire? Is your internal dialogue with yourself very harsh? ... *Look at the ball! Stand more sideways! Start on time! Typical, you are just too slow. Why don't you concentrate? Serves you right, you did not train enough. Idiot! Damn racket! Playing into the sun, hopeless!* ... Would you allow anyone to talk to you like that? Would you suffer quietly and just take the punishment you deserve? Maybe you would fire this coach? Your chances to win are 1:100, if you cut yourself down in this manner. You don't have confidence in yourself. And you likely don't react this way on the tennis court only. You probably order yourself around in the office in the same way. You complain when your competitor takes one of your orders. You punish yourself with disdain, treat yourself like an idiot and don't have faith in yourself when it comes to anything beyond your daily routine.

When you are standing in front of a display of that crazy expensive car of your dreams, what kind of voice do you hear? ... *You'll be driving this car, and sooner than you think.* ... Or do you tend to hear. ... *How do you want to pay for that? You need a new refrigerator, the rent is going up and the kids want new ski equipment. What are you thinking? With your pitiful salary? You'll never get there!* ... Then do you go on with strong and determined steps, or are you depressed and unsure of yourself?

The inner vampire is spiteful and sly. He knows your most secret weaknesses. He knows how to hurt you. You can't lie to him. He never leaves you alone, not at night, not in your dreams. You wake up with him and you go to sleep with him. He knows your most secret hopes and your most secret sins. Nonetheless he is not invincible.

There are three strategies for dealing with your inner vampire in an effective way – how to go from being a vampire to becoming your own friend. You will find these strategies in Simply Do It 8 through 10.

5.5 Simply Do It 8: Become a friend to your fellow man

You can begin in your family. Just listen to yourself. If you're brave enough record yourself when you are talking to your partner or your children. You will shudder. You will hear a person who knows everything better, a person who never encourages anyone, only hands out orders and has little or no understanding for the worries and hopes of his children. This alone should suffice as a introduction to the exercise.

This assignment fits well with your temporary abstinence from television, since you will have gained the necessary time. Listen and try to learn. Once in a while remember that you, too, were young once. Meet your children's or your partner's ideas positively. Support your family in their own development and in trying something new.

> **NOW** say something nice to someone in your family. Say ... *I like you as a person* ... to your son or daughter, ... *I am proud of you* ... , ... *I am glad you are here* ... . Tell your partner ... *I love you* ... , ... *I am happy that I have you.* ...

Do you feel your resistance to these simple sentences? Do you feel how unfamiliar this is for you? It is sad that you find it hard to be nice. There always has to be a special reason for you to be halfway caring. If your partner or one of your children were to have an accident, then you would get sentimental and bemoan all the missed opportunities. Why not act now? Why wait until it is too late? Do it now! **Do it now!**

CALL your parents and thank them. Don't make it a big deal. It does not have to be an invitation to the opera and dinner where you can say some formal words of thanks while raising a glass of champagne. Do it now, and say that you had to call now that you realized how much your parents have done for you. Or send an email, or a letter. The important thing is that you act now. If you don't do it now, you never will. By the way: if you feel like inviting your parents to the opera, why not? But thank them first, right now. Tomorrow might be too late.

Next time you are sitting around with your friends, pay attention to how the conversation develops. When the mood seems to drop, when the pack gangs up on one in the group who was stupid enough to express his idea or to utter a word of hope, then remember that now your time has come. Take a clear stance in favor of the idea, say verbatim (you might not have the words at hand at the time, but that should not stop you):

> ... THAT sounds good. Of course it could work. One can always work out the details. I think it's a great idea, and very courageous. ...

Now enjoy the difference. You give your energy as a friend and, to your surprise, you will find that you are getting stronger for it. If you don't block your energy but you let it flow, you'll connect with a stream of energy. Don't take this as a mystical remark – just test it out.

If you don't get it right the first time, but tantalizingly get swept up in the general slaughter of ideas, don't give up. As soon as you become aware of it, make the switch. The goal is clear.

Don't be a vampire. Be a friend.

5.6 Simply Do It 9: Change the tone of your inner voice

The next time you hear your own nagging inner voice order you around, berate you or put you down, do something totally out of the ordinary. Take sides with yourself, clearly and without restriction. If the voice begins to blame you for everything and anyone that brings trouble, be your own protector. Stand up for yourself without hesitation. If the voice scolds you because you don't make enough money while everyone is buying a new car, going on luxury vacations, showing off their Rolex or mobile device, it might just sound like this (before your Simply To Do) ... *You just don't earn enough. Whatever you do, it doesn't work out. Don't you see how everyone else is getting a promotion while your career is at a standstill? Why don't you try harder?* ... Now here is your challenge (just do it):

> ... You are doing well. Everything is going to be okay. Just stay calm and trust in your goals. Whatever you do, don't give up. I am proud of you!
> ...

Do you feel the enormous difference? Do you feel your shoulders relax, like the fear is falling away and the pressure is dropping?

At first the tone is not that easy to get right. You are probably not used to providing support in a calm and concentrated way. Do this as if, for example, it is part of your job that you often have to deal with people who are afraid, for example as a nurse or caregiver or kindergarden teacher, i.e. the way they talk to insecure patients or children, to quiet their fear, to calm them and protect them.

Remarkably, many people immediately grasp this method spontaneously as a key element in achieving far-reaching changes in their lives. They immediately recognize that their problems stem directly from how they handle themselves. An overly critical, nagging attitude towards yourself will surely lead to precisely the same kind of attitude towards others. If you are not good enough for yourself you will readily criticize others, too. As a survival technique, this is quite understandable. Who could bear it all the time that others are okay, nice people with small faults, while seeing oneself as inadequate and bad?

It is said that you should love your neighbor as yourself. This can also mean love yourself as you love your neighbor. Maybe it is intended to be not so much a command as an observation: If you don't love yourself, you cannot love others.

Again you will run into your ego. It will resist. It will prefer a harsher tone. Maybe you have rarely received loving support during your life. Maybe the tone in your home was strict rather than caring. This means you will have little experience available for you to fall back on. Accordingly, your ego will see a sizable risk in accepting unknown strategies. This is understandable and it is not intended take away your stability.

Just like the entire Start Living! 6 week training, this exercise is also intended to be an experiment. Just test it out and decide to use this method, as it is proven to work, and will give you more security and support you better. This is not about a unique, guaranteed technique based on a one size fits all type of formula. This is about your very own, personal learning experiences. You will find your path, your own version with which you will feel comfortable and achieve better results than before.

5.7 Simply Do It 10: Cut off the serpent's head

In some very tough cases it may prove to be more healing to fight the inner voice with all your might. When doubt and fear seem to be overwhelming, cut off that inner voice with determination and make the decision for success and support for yourself. Remember that at least during the 6 week training period of the Start Living! program you do not want anyone near you who will weaken you, scorn your goals, judge your chances negatively or with pessimism, or treat you carelessly in general. Don't tolerate this from yourself, either.

When your inner voice speaks to you while you are falling asleep, during the night, or in the early morning: ... *You can't do it. It won't work out. You cannot change this.* ... Then say to yourself, out loud. ... *Of course I can do it. There is no doubt. I am loved by life and supported by life. Everything is going to be okay.* ...

You don't necessarily have to say it out loud. It is enough if you do it forcefully in your thoughts. Get that inner voice to shut up. Cut off the serpent's head!

Life prefers positive tendencies. Life prefers prosperity, health and happiness. As soon as you set those tendencies in gear they automatically become stronger. You must not try to force change into your life – that would be a mistake. What does a gardener do when he plants a flower? Can he make the flower grow? He relies on the power living within the seed. He only needs to start the process by giving it a suitable environment. The flower will seize the smallest opportunity to grow. If the gardener thinks that he can trigger or accelerate this process with his own power, if he tugs and pulls on the plant, he will destroy it. Only experimentation with the environmental conditions and consistent patience will lead to the desired result.

If you concentrate on the positive tendencies you will strengthen them. In this way you give fate clear order. ... *I want this to turn out well. I won't have a different result.* ... This is the only language that fate understands. Clear instructions spoken with authority will bring clear results. It is not your strength that creates the results. It is in your instructions to bundle the latent tendencies which are already there and to give them a clear direction – this is how you get the results you want.

If you find yourself in a situation which seems really difficult, maybe even hopeless, it takes a considerable amount of courage to decide for rescue from this situation. It is possible that the next few days might bring financial misfortune, that you are seemingly at the end of your rope in terms of your health, that your personal relationship falls apart, or that you have to face some other serious blow from fate. The external circumstances could be staggering. You are probably asking yourself ... *Is there any hope left? Is there any way out for me?* ...

It can also be that you were told that there is no longer a humanly possible way out. The balance sheet may be crushing and your debt is high. ... *It's all over, bankruptcy is all that is left.* ... The doctor's test results may be devastating and paint a hopeless picture. ... *Hopeless, incurable.* ... Maybe you suffer with being overweight and have given up all hope of feeling comfortable in the company of others, being part of the group, having fun. ... *Not me, I can't do it. I will never be one of them.* ... Maybe you no longer have the strength to believe in a satisfying personal relationship ... *I am not attractive enough. It's not meant to be for me. I am too old. ...*

It's never too late. No situation is hopeless. Creation has succeeded in creating billions of stars, keeping these stars in a powerful balance of forces, and it has the power and the energy to solve your problem too. There is no difference between large and small problems. Never give up!

It's never too late.

5.8 In the meanwhile

You are working on your goals. You are working on your trust in yourself, on your belief that you can achieve these goals, and life's readiness to give you everything you want. Now what you need is the persistence to keep at it for a while. The next chapter is devoted to this subject.

5.9 Summary

The second dimension: trust and confidence

As soon as you have worked out your goals, the most important requirement to reach them is to build trust: YOU create your life. YOU have your fate in your hands. This is why you will certainly reach your goals.

The following Simply Do It assignments will serve to increase your trust in life step by step so that you grow with the certainty that you are loved by life.

Simply Do It 5: Building confidence

Shut out the negative brainwashing of the mass media completely for the next 6 weeks: do not watch television and do not read a newspaper. Ever!

Instead, focus on the people you love and the subjects which promote your goals. Actively use the time you have gained for your family and friends. Read books and magazines that deal with subjects related to your personal goals.

Simply Do It 6: Immerse yourself in your goals

Invest yourself consciously in books and magazines dealing with subjects relating to your personal goals.

Simply Do It 7: Avoid energy vampires

To build up your confidence, you have to increase your positive mental energy. To do this avoid anyone who systematically robs you of your energy and enthusiasm for the next 6 weeks.

Simply Do It 8: Be a friend to your fellow man

Spare yourself the negative remarks and the criticism and say nice and caring things instead. Say: ... *I like you ... I love you ... I am happy you are here,* ... etc. Praise and give thanks. Support others in their ideas. Share love, strength and courage. Be a friend. Start in your family.

Simply Do It 9: Change the tone of your inner voice

Take the fight to your own inner energy vampire. Pay attention to your inner voice and give it a new tone and content from now on. Speak to yourself the same way you would expect to be spoken to by your best friend. Be nice and caring to yourself, and give yourself strength and courage.

Simply Do It 10: Cut off the serpent's head

On the path to reaching our goals our greatest enemy is ourselves and that negative inner voice. Defend yourself, strongly if necessary. If the voice surfaces within your internal dialog, like an evil serpent, telling you that you can't do it, just imagine cutting off the serpent's head. Silence it, and keep doing this over and over forever. You are loved by life and life wants you to reach your goals. It is never too late! Protect yourself from anything that seems to go against this. Never, never ever give up.

6 The Third Dimension: Persistence

The spirit is willing, but the flesh is weak. This famous quotation from the Gospel of Matthew and the Gospel of Mark seems to color our efforts in realizing a more conscious existence. Habits are tough to beat and cannot be eradicated with good intentions alone.

Persistence itself is also a habit which may be cultivated just like any other habit. If we practice persistence with simple things, it can then be generally applied to more difficult areas. In addition, we should be aware that persistence is often confused with the absence of errors and therefore seems to be virtually unattainable.

6.1 The difference between winners and losers

Among the most widespread and most grave errors in general opinion is this misunderstanding: whoever wants to be successful is not allowed to make mistakes. People who want to quit smoking can never smoke another cigarette. Those who've decided to go running regularly cannot take a break for a week. A good student can never fail. A successful entrepreneur never starts a project that goes wrong. The list is as long as it is false.

Persistence means sticking with your goals. It does not mean having no setbacks.

It does not mean you don't have to overcome any difficulties. In fact, setbacks actually are so very typical for successful people that they deserve an explanation:

The difference between winners and losers is not that winners never lose. The difference is that winners get over their losses faster.

Winners get back up faster and more often. Losers give up more quickly; they doubt and despair; they capitulate for all kinds of reasons:

Losers give up because they no longer believe that their goals can be achieved. ... *It's not possible. I can't do it. I was wrong. ...*

Losers give up because they believe they cannot take the stress any longer. ... *It doesn't make sense. It's not worth it. ...*

Losers give up because they doubt themselves. ... *I bit off more than I can chew. I was too sure of myself.* ...

Losers give up because they fear risking failure. ... *I will be desperate. I will regret this. Everything will have been in vain.* ...

Losers give up because they think more about the opinions from the world around them than they do about their own goals. ... *What would my friends say? I will die of embarrassment.* ...

Losers give up because they believe that real winners are not allowed to have any problems, know no fears and never fail. ... *If I'm already thinking of quitting now, I'll never make it. I wasn't made for this, I get scared too quickly.* ...

Losers give up before they even start. ... *It's not possible. I won't be able to do it. I'll regret it. I would just embarrass myself.* ...

Winners have learned to handle setbacks. They don't give up. They remain true to their goals, even if (and especially if) the goals seem to be unattainable. They count on running into problems. They know, however, that it's exactly those problems which separate the wheat from the chaff. Losers see any difficulty as an inevitable stop sign: do not advance. Winners solve problems differently; they approach them more like stations in a fitness program, for example as individual exercises. Winners know that overcoming problems increases the probability of reaching the goal. Losers tend to view the same problem as a sign that the goal cannot be reached.

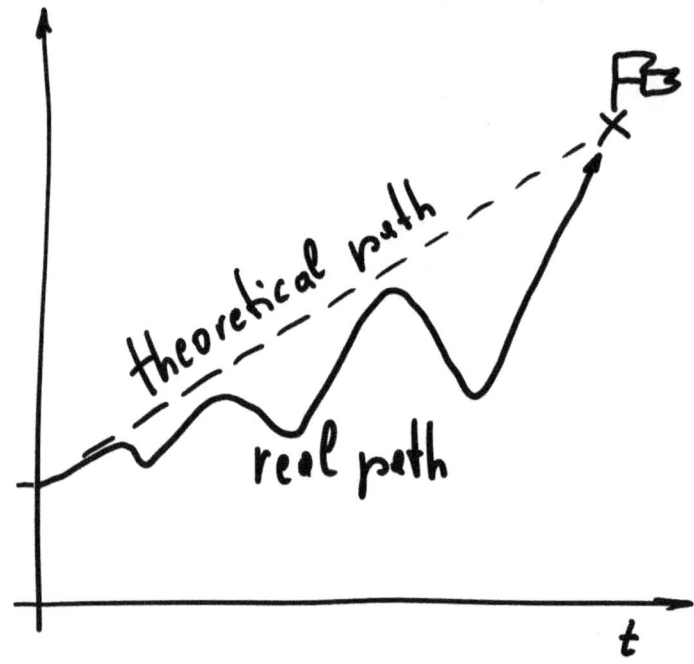

Of course it would be nice if the path to our goals were always straight. For big goals, that is seldom the case. The path to your goal runs across clearly uneven territory, over many or few hard setbacks.

Every one of those obstacles can trigger you to give up. Every one of these setbacks can also be a step that makes you stronger, trains your willpower and moves the goal closer.

Recognizing this connection is the first step toward persistence. Problems are much like dumbbells at the gym. If you lift a light one you will have a very positive perception of how strong you are. You tend to over-estimate your progress. If you lift a heavy weight you have to struggle much harder, but you will also make progress more quickly. Every single ounce of weight encourages your muscles to grow. To reach the same results using a light weight, you will have to increase your number of repetitions until you have reached your limit, just as you do when using heavy weights. Only when you are at your limits will you achieve progress. Without weight – no muscle growth! **Without problems – no success!** The same equation and the same connection.

Problems are never insurmountable obstacles which keep you from reaching your goals. Never! Just the mere fact that you believe in a goal makes it attainable. Goals can find their own ways of being attainable. Intense thoughts have a strong tendency to manifest. As soon as you set a desire in motion and charge it with energy through repetition and strong emotional involvement, it will push to be realized. Unstoppable, and with the same quiet patience of the river which builds up behind an obstacle until the pressure has grown so strong that it demolishes the obstacle. In the end, nothing can stop its flow toward the ocean.

Persistence means that you remain true to your goal. Regardless of whether you look good or bad in the eyes of onlookers, you stick with your dreams. You know that difficulties are weights; they are there so you can develop your strength as quickly as possible. When there are setbacks, you just ask yourself what you can learn from them.

If you have grasped this idea, you will begin to enjoy the challenges. You know that through those problems, you get there faster. You compare your challenges to a bungee cord and your goal to the point where the cord is connected. When the cord is under the most tension it also has the greatest force to retract. It will catapult you back up quickly with force after reaching its lowest point. There is only a single possibility of preventing this turnaround and to really fall. For this to happen, you would have to cut the cord and sever the connection to the anchoring point. That is when your deepest fears would come true. You would drop to your death and the crowd, standing by in anticipation, would have something to talk about. Overcome by shudders of delight, they could talk about someone who wanted to be so clever. Arrogance comes before the fall – the television audience would be congratulated on staying safe. Best to stick with what you know. The brief good feeling of knowing they were right leaves the audience with a new highlight of their week.

It wasn't the tautness of the rope or the growing distance from the anchoring point which led to the failure. It was entirely the decision to throw in the towel and give up.

In the same way, you cannot distance yourself from your goal; you cannot lose sight of it, even if times get tough. You have never been closer to the fulfillment of your dreams. Ask yourself the crucial question from the section about confidence. ... *Does life want me to reach my goals? Does life want me to fulfill my purpose?* ...

And if your ego sets a trap for you in one last desperate attempt – ... *What if it your destiny is failure?* ... – then, imaging taking a big sword, a sword so big that you need two hands, and cut off the serpent's head. You are loved by life and life will never, never, never ever want you to fail. This single decision has to be made by you, and things will go your way again. The setback is over. You will feel a surge immediately after you make that decision. It is only a matter of this one decision. You decide that you are loved by life – and that's it.

The depth of the low depends exclusively on your ability to make this single decision. As long as you are uncertain of this decision, the results will be uncertain, and the ups and downs of your path can be like a roller-coaster. If you gain more and more control over your thoughts by consistently following the rules from the Start Living! 6 week training, there will be fewer low points and they will be less intense. As soon as you see one coming, meet it with the certainty that your goals will not be changed and you may suffer a little and maybe have a harder time than you would like, but you will go through it more quickly and get back on your planned course.

6.2 Simply Do It 11: Decide upon something simple and follow through

Persistence and riding a bike have several things in common. In theory both are very simple. We cannot imagine an operating manual for either riding a bicycle or being persistent. Sit down, keep your balance and start pedaling – that's all there is to bicycle riding. Special techniques are reserved for pros who have to endure long and/or highly demanding rides and still make good time. It is similar with persistence. **Follow through with the things you set out to do.** There is nothing more to it. Persistence is learned much like riding a bicycle, by doing. Any other attempts are useless. One can get some help at the beginning, and a few tips might be useful. Other than that, there is just this simple rule: Just do it.

> EACH day follow through with something simple that you have clearly intended to do. It does not have to be anything especially good, no special performance or earning of recognition. This is only about showing your subconscious that the things which you claim to be making happen in the morning actually come to pass.

Persistence is learned through consistent action. So how do you begin if you have never been consistent? The fallacy lies in this self-evaluation. Most people are pretty consistent, although not in all things they wished they were. They consistently forget what they intended to do. They consistently let every little thing distract them. They consistently drive their car, even for the shortest of trips. They consistently turn on the television every evening.

However, these consistent acts are not seen as an accomplishment because they are without effort. None of the noted attitudes require any work. Nevertheless, they show an impressive consistency. If the television breaks down even the most apathetic among us can take decisive action and make efforts to solve this problem. Repair services are contracted even during nighttime hours and a long repair time will only be accepted if a replacement TV will be provided. If a habit is interrupted, it leads to immediate withdrawal symptoms which are experienced as being painful. This pain motivates the affected people.

Relatedly, to prepare for a more consciously consistent life, it is helpful to make use of this latent tendency to be consistent and to maintain habits. The exercise above is designed to serve this purpose. If you have a habit of drinking one to two glasses of wine every night, then decide in the morning whether you will drink one or two glasses of wine. In the evening stick to your decision. Drink the exact amount, no more and no less. Hold this fact in your conscious mind, briefly but clearly. ... *That's what I decided, and that's what it's going to be!* ...

If you decide in the morning that you are going to the movies that evening, then follow through on your decision. ... *That's what I decided, and that's what it's going to be!* ...

If you decide to write a letter today, then take care of it today. Not tomorrow and not the day after. ... *That's what I decided and that's how it's going to be!* ...

The trick is to decide to do things which are simple enough so that they can be easily taken care of, and then to be consciously aware of the completion. The way your subconscious operates is uncomplicated. It is not intellectual and knows no ranking of difficulties. It simply is aware of what happens. If you always talk big and then don't follow through, your subconscious will pick up on that as a rule. It knows no consequences, good or bad, successful or not. The subconscious, which directs universal forces, is always successful because it always achieves what it perceives as your goal. However, it does not learn those things we talk about – it learns from our feelings and our actions.

If someone is unhappy with his job and feels underpaid he will likely test his displeasure out at home from time to time. ... *I can't take it anymore. Tomorrow I'll demand higher wages. It can't go on like this. That's enough.* ... This decision creates energy. During the drive to work in the morning the first doubts arise. ... *What if I'm turned down? What if they suggest I work somewhere else or if they just fire me on the spot? I'm easily replaced.* ... So when going through the door at work all the boldness and courage is gone. He changes over into his usual internal dialogue of resignation. In front of his friends at the bar, the whole thing is described as a glorious victory. ... *I am not that stupid to give them a chance to let me go. They'd like that just fine. No, I am too smart for that. They cannot manipulate me into this. Ha, I showed them.* ...

What should the subconscious of this person learn from this story other than all talk and no action. Then, when there really is a serious situation one day, when very real and necessary action is required, the subconscious will torpedo any attempts. ... *Sure, you'll follow through! It's the same every time. Big talk and then... nothing! It will be like that again.* ... The urgently required connection to our abundant available life energy cannot take place.

Please keep in mind that the subconscious does not do this out of revenge or ill will. It obeys habit. It has learned that things are connected as follows: big intentions and zero follow-through. With every small or large project that you carry out sloppily, you feed into this vicious circle.

Over the years many people have developed a habit of not following through. They are impressively consistently inconsistent. This learning experience of the subconscious leads to painful effects when it comes to big goals and big plans. ... *I won't get upset as much. I will delegate more. I will lose weight. I will not lie to my partner. I won't smoke anymore. I won't drive after drinking anymore, I will, I will, I will.* ... An unending procession of New Year's resolutions full of honest intentions yet without results because they are shot down by our own inner strength which is endlessly superior to any external efforts we may make.

Through daily steps of following through on small plans, you can turn this effect around. This is how your subconscious brings your goal more and more in harmony with its power. Remember that your subconscious does not have to change anything per se. It has always carried out what you, its lord and master, have told it to do. If you change your strategy now and you would like to follow up on your words with deeds, this will be accepted without delay. That's how it's going to be; that is the only way for the subconscious to react. Instead of "big intentions, zero implementation", now it is "every intention is followed by an action" – no emotion, no criticism and obedient.

DECIDE now on some small, insignificant thing you can immediately carry out. For example: now I'll go drink a glass of water. After you have made this conscious decision, get up and manifest this decision. Drink a glass of water. Notice your reaction. Maybe you felt resistance to this process, which may actually be camouflaged as discerning intelligence (I don't take orders from a book!) or agreement (I will do straight away.), which in reality only shows once again your powerlessness in the face of your habit of not following through. Maybe you will have a feeling of power which comes up when you document what you are truly capable of.

Don't underestimate the power of this exercise. It is really amazing that we humans are capable of manifesting our thoughts in reality. It is completely unclear how this works. The greatest thinkers in the world have pondered this question, while each one of us just simply does it. Thoughts become reality. You think about getting up and – voila – you get up. Did you know that first there was the thought, something unfathomable, without weight, invisible, free? Now, only seconds later, this reality has movement and your material body and then the nonliving matter such as the water faucet and a glass have actually obeyed this apparently weak impulse. Millions of nerve and muscle impulses had to be coordinated to bring about this seemingly natural performance, to lift up an unstable body on its two legs, to make it fill a glass with water and then to drink the water. We don't even realize what a miracle this is because we are so used to it. Let's put ourselves into the shoes of someone who is not capable of these actions because he seems to be too ill to do this. He will see this as a miracle if he were suddenly able to do it. Nonetheless, after a short while he would be used to it again and would return to his usual thoughts, and grumble as before, ungrateful and thoughtless.

>CALL someone right now who you can thank. Call somebody who will be happy about this call. Just decide and manifest it! Right now!

A common ego trap worth mentioning: ... *I will do it perfectly. But right now I don't have time for it. I don't like to do things halfway.* ... Don't think you have to be admirable now. It's not that your expectations of yourself are too high, but that your ego has a firm grip on you. Just do it! Act! Take action now! How many letters were never written because you never had time for the perfect one? How many phone calls have you never made because there was only a minute of time? Every lost opportunity is a shame. These opportunities never return.

Before you fall into sentimental self-pity, you had better recognize that you are wasting time again if you do that. Take action now! If you are sending an email to encourage someone, to show him or her that you are thinking of them, then you have performed a miracle. You have mastered your own inner weakness. You have outwitted a habit. You have shown your subconscious how things will be going from now on. And even if you never again send a letter or an email, this time will be forever etched in your memory. You did it. You moved the world. Not out of blind habit, not out of tradition, not due to some rule, but out of your own decision to follow the advice from a book. Soon you will no longer need the book and its advice.

6.3 Simply To Do 12: The love letter project

There is one feeling so powerful that it can change absolutely any situation for the better. This feeling is called gratitude. There is no condition which cannot be changed by an intense feeling of gratitude.

Gratitude is capable of radically shortening the time required to reach a certain goal. It enables your subconscious to wipe out years of habits and limitations which have seemed overwhelming so far.

Gratitude is an incredible concept and yet it is easily explained. When you are grateful it means that you have already received. There is no doubt. When you give thanks, the original problem is over. ... *I give thanks for the help I received.* ... Can you feel the difference compared to a request? ... *I'm asking you to help me.* ...

A plea, a request contains a bit of fear, which is fed by two sources.

First, to ask means that it is quite possible that your request might be denied. If this were not so, you would not have to ask. It is not a matter of politeness, but rather a fundamental inner attitude. If you want to instruct fate and embellish your request with the word "please", that's okay. If you ask, plead or beg, your subconscious will gather from this that the outcome is uncertain. Accordingly, the results will be uncertain as well. Sometimes your requests will be fulfilled, sometimes they won't. Results vary from time to time.

Second, a request indicates lack, i.e. that you have not yet received something. That is not a good starting position from a mental point of view. He who has will receive, he who has not, will have things taken from him. This means that you have to take up an internal position which says you "have". Only then will you receive. A request essentially contradicts this principle.

You can avoid both of these mental problems with the feeling of gratitude. When you give thanks, you have already received. It cannot be refused. It is no longer an estimation in the sense that it will not be refused, but a definite statement of absolute certainty. I have already received it. It is done. It is taken care of. In this way you clarify that you already have and therefore you will receive.

> THE "Love Letter Project": Once a week you will write a love letter. This means you write a letter thanking somebody for something you have experienced within the past few days. It must be a letter that includes no expectations in return. When this letter is in reference to someone in a business, you will write the letter to upper management with the request to forward your thanks to the respective party.

On Friday, don't leave the office to go home before you have written your love letter. Recap the events of the week and decide on one person who stands out in your mind. If you cannot think of anyone, if that whole week long there was no one you noticed, this should give you something to think about. You have probably gone through the week with blinders on. You probably did not really pay attention to anyone. You probably did not thank anyone. You likely took everything for granted. You probably did not react in a kind and loving way, not once, and you gave nothing back. You live in one of the richest parts of the world and you didn't even notice.

Can you remember something that was not perfect – something you found annoying? It's a safe bet that you will remember something right away. You had to wait in line at the cash register. At the subway station you got upset when you saw a few rude kids. Gas prices have gone up. One of the people you work with was sick. One of your kids played hooky from school or you had a cough, or a sore throat, or something else that can give you the opportunity to be upset.

Could it be that this is really all that remained of your life from an entire week? If later on you want to tell your grandchildren about your life, will you share these highlights of nonsense? ... Tell us a story from when you were young. ... ... *Well, I was really upset because gas prices went up.* ... Are you kidding?

You really can't remember a moment when you received good service, when people were patient and polite even 10 minutes before closing time, when a gas station attendant gave you good service in the middle of the night, despite the bitter cold. Not one time did you say thank you, you really helped me a lot. Are you one of those people who thinks it is to be expected that everything goes well? Will you mention it only when something goes wrong? Well then, good night. Your poor colleagues, partner and children are to be pitied. Those self-sacrificing victims who have to suffer under your reign deserve our complete sympathy. In this case, the only consolation is the fact that you are no better off. Rarely do you receive any praise. Few people would really like you. It's a shame, the wonderful life you are unable to enjoy in such a way.

You should never again in your lifetime let a week slip away like that. It is a shame to let those few years pass by in criticism, cynicism and self-righteousness. Weeks like that make you old, wrinkled and ugly. Nothing else remarkable has happened, only that you got a little older, uglier and more wrinkled.

Therefore, the course of action is quite clear. You buy a few sheets of stationary and go to work on them once a week. You write your personal LLP (Love Letter Project). Over the course of time you will write to oil companies, department stores, boutiques, car dealerships, schools and hospitals, to other participants from seminars, book publishers, magazine editors and airlines. Among the millions of letters which are often sent, yours will be among the few which clearly carry a positive message.

This way you are documenting an entirely different attitude. You are concentrating on the positive, on the enjoyable. You reward yourself as well as the recipient of the letter. Sometimes you'll receive a reply, but most of the time you won't. Through this project you are changing your vibration and the results will return to you very quickly. Total strangers will smile at you and you will smile back. You will receive gifts and give gifts, and you really can't be sure which is more enjoyable.

You will never want to change this. Once you know what you have been missing, you will not want to trade places for a single week, or day, or hour with that old person you were before who shuffled with a closed mind through the day.

Welcome to life!

6.4 Summary

To reach our goals we only need more persistence and confidence. Then our goals will show up like the closing of a prayer.

To change our life we have to change our habits. Habits are changed through persistence. Persistence itself is a habit that we can train.

Persistence means holding steadfast to your goals. It does not mean you never make mistakes, nor does it mean you never have setbacks. Setbacks and mistakes are quite normal. Only those who do nothing make no mistakes.

Winners fall down as many times as losers do, but they get up more quickly and they keep getting up. Losers stay down and give up.

Simply Do It 11: Decide on something simple and follow through

Learn to be persistent. Persistence is learned through doing and not by thinking about it. Every day decide to do one simple thing and follow through exactly as you have planned it. If you decide to drink one glass of wine, drink exactly one. This is how your subconscious learns that you are persistent and that you are reliable. It learns that you are capable of getting things done.

Simply Do It 12: The Love Letter Project

Learn to be grateful. Gratitude is the most helpful and most effective feeling on your path to reaching your goal. Practice being thankful, as well as being aware of the countless positive things you experience daily. Once a week write a "love letter". Write it to someone who helped you; it might be someone in your family, a friend or someone at a business you visited. Give thanks and expect nothing in return. This is how you direct your attention to the positive aspects and that will change your life for the better.

www.ingramcontent.com/pod-product-compliance
Lightning Source LLC
Chambersburg PA
CBHW070452090426
42735CB00012B/2524